Are You Happy: Finding the CEO in YOU

Finding the CEO in YOU

Copyright © 2023 by Trient Press

All rights reserved. No part of this publication may be reproduced, distributed, or transmitted in any form or by any means, including photocopying, recording, or other electronic or mechanical methods, without the prior written permission of the publisher, except in the case of brief quotations embodied in critical reviews and certain other noncommercial uses permitted by copyright law. For permission requests, write to the publisher, addressed "Attention: Permissions Coordinator," at the address below.

Criminal copyright infringement, including infringement without monetary gain, is investigated by the FBI and is punishable by up to five years in federal prison and a fine of $250,000.

Except for the original story material written by the author, all songs, song titles, and lyrics mentioned in the novel 18 Steps to Excellence are the exclusive property of the respective artists, songwriters, and copyright holder.

Trient Press
3375 S Rainbow Blvd
#81710, SMB 13135
Las Vegas,NV 89180

Ordering Information:
Quantity sales. Special discounts are available on quantity purchases by corporations, associations, and others. For details, contact the publisher at the address above.
Orders by U.S. trade bookstores and wholesalers. Please contact Trient Press:
   Tel: (775) 996-3844; or visit www.trientpress.com.
   Printed in the United States of America
   Publisher's Cataloging-in-Publication data
Ruscsak, M.L
A title of a book : Are You Happy: Finding the CEO in You

ISBN
E-book	978-1-955198-77-6
Paperback	978-1-955198-76-9
Hard Cover	978-1-955198-75-2

Forward

It is my honor to write the foreword for this groundbreaking book that delves into the realm of personal and professional effectiveness. In a world where technological advancements are rapidly changing the way we live, work, and connect, it is more important than ever to cultivate a set of skills and behaviors that enable us to thrive in this ever-evolving landscape.

Melisa's journey has been far from easy, often hindered by her self-doubt and insecurity, unbeknownst to me, it wasn't until 2017 that a turning point came in the form of a question I asked her, during an interview. "What is holding you back?" This question led Melisa on a path of self-enlightenment and healing, using my book, "So Happy and Grateful" as a guide to finding her own compass.

As a polymath with expertise in multiple fields, I understand the power of effective communication, empathy, and self-awareness in shaping our future. Through my work on the Master Algorithm and my mission to create 100,000 millionaires and give back $1.5 billion by 2025, I am constantly reminded of the importance of putting first things first and developing a winning mentality.

Are You Happy: Finding the CEO in YOU is a treasure trove of insights and strategies that will help you to become the best version of yourself and transform your life and business. From working from home and lifestyle design to leadership strategies and personal growth, this book covers all the critical components of effectiveness. The author's depth of knowledge and ability to communicate complex ideas in an easy-to-understand manner is genuinely inspiring.

As you embark on this journey, I encourage you to stay motivated and stay on track. The path to effectiveness and success is not easy, but with hard work, dedication, and a commitment to growth, you can achieve your goals and make a positive impact on the world.

Finding the CEO in YOU

Thank you for taking the time to read this book, and I hope you find it as valuable as I have. Let's continue to shape the future and live in the light and love of the one infinite creator.

Best,
Antonio T. Smith Jr, CEO of Arlingbrook Social Media, Innovative Technologist, and Melisa's number one fan.

Are You Happy

Table of Contents:

Note From The Author

Part I
Emerging Effectiveness

Chapter 1	The Basics On Effectiveness
Chapter 2	Be Proactive
Chapter 3	Clarify Your Goals
Chapter 4	Learn To Put First Things First
Chapter 5	Understand The Win Win Mentality
Chapter 6	Learn Empathy
Chapter 7	The Benefits Of Being A More Effective Person
Chapter 8	Staying Motivated To be More Effective
Chapter 9	Staying On Track
Chapter 10	Making Resolutions For Being An Effective Person

Part II
Become the Best Version of Yourself

Chapter 11	Being Yourself

Assessing Yourself

Chapter 12	Projecting Yourself
Chapter 13	Learning Your Triggers
Chapter 14	Knocking Down Your Barriers

Rejection

Injustice

Humiliation

Abandonment

Betrayal (or Treason)

Chapter 15	Create Boundaries
Chapter 16	Increase Your Self-Confidence and Self-Esteem

Finding the CEO in YOU

Self-Confidence
Self-Esteem
Appreciate Yourself
Be Proud of Your Accomplishments
Recognize Your Skill
Learn to Love Your Body

Chapter 17	Connecting with Your Authenticity
Chapter 18	Reconnecting with Your Inner Child
Chapter 19	Tame Your Inner Voice
Chapter 20	Increase Your Self-Awareness

Your Thoughts

Part III
Business & Life Transformations

Chapter 21	Working From Home

The Possible Health Benefits
The Health Risks
Working From Home:
What You Will Learn

Chapter 22	Create your 'Smart' Lifestyle Design

Digital Nomad? Or Digital Homebody
What is a Digital Nomad?
Unchain Yourself
An Introduction to Lifestyle Design
Preparing for Your Journey
Go Online for Remote Jobs
Start Your Own Online Business or Micro Business

Chapter 23	Set-Up your Work Culture

Your Work Environment

Are You Happy

Setting Up a 'Mobile Command Center'
Creating Your Home Office
Some Health Tips for Working at a Computer

Chapter 24 — Staying Discipline

Accepting Work
Choosing Clients
Revenue Streams
Targets
Systems
Hypothesis Testing
Your Personal Life

Chapter 25 — Optimizing Performance, Health and Productivity

Optimizing Sleep
Exercise
Nutrition
Introducing Kaizen

Chapter 26 — Home Business Models

Top Home Business Models for Lifestyle Design
Section Thoughts
Notes

Part IV
The Expert In You
How to Find Your Expertise
How to Monetize on Your Expertise

Part V
Pursue You Passion

Chapter 27 — Find Your Passion
Chapter 28 — Find Your Passion's Skill Set
Chapter 29 — Scale Your Passion
Chapter 30 — Live Your Passion with Intention
Addendum: True Stories

Finding the CEO in YOU

Part VI
Leadership Strategies

Introduction

Chapter 31	Everyday Leadership and How it Can Improve Your Life
Chapter 32	The Truth About Leadership
Chapter 33	Key Skills of Leaders and Self Assessment
Chapter 34	Leading Without the Title
Chapter 35	Lead Yourself to Success with the Grow Model
Chapter 36	Self-Awareness and Personal Growth
Chapter 37	Be an Inspiring Agent of Change
Chapter 38	Barriers to Leadership
Chapter 39	Blueprint to Develop Your Leadership Skills
Chapter 40	Being a Good Leader to Becoming a Great Leader
Skill 1:	Communication
Skill 2:	Adaptability
Skill 3:	Team Building
Skill 4:	Strategic Thinking
Skill 5:	Delegation

Extras

Part VII
Choose to Lead

Introduction

Chapter 1:	Everyday Leadership and how it can improve your life
Chapter 2:	The Truth About Leadership
Chapter 3:	Key Skills of Leaders and Self-

Are You Happy

Assessment
Strategic Thinking
Inspiring and Motivating
Critical Thinking, Analyzing and Problem-Solving Abilities
Demonstrating Transparency, Integrity, and Honesty
Developing Others
Learning, Creating and Innovating
Driving Results
Communicating in a Powerful and Effective Way
Building Relationships
Displaying Technical or Professional Expertise

Chapter 4: Leading Without the Title
Values

Chapter 5: Lead Yourself to Success With the Grow Model
What Is The GROW Model?
GOAL (G)
REALITY (R)
OPTIONS (O)
WILL (W)

Chapter 6: Self-Awareness and Personal Growth
Chapter 7: Be an Inspiring Agent of Change
Chapter 8: Barriers to Leadership
Being Open to Feedback
Moving Into Action
Accepting Responsibility for Mistakes
Facing Disagreement
Confidence When Facing Failure
Maintaining Focus
Humility Versus Success

Chapter 9: Learn When to Step Aside
Blueprint to Develop Your Leadership Skills
Practice mindfulness

Are You Happy

Note from the Author:

My path has never been easy. Most of the time it was myself, that got in my own way. However, it wasn't until 2017 that I began to understand what the issues were.

Thanks to my now mentor Antonio T. Smith. Jr and his one question that he asked me after an interview, I begun my journey to self enlightenment. So what was the question that he asked? "What is holding you back?"

Following his guidance in his then new book "So Happy and Grateful" I found the stepping stones I needed to start to heal. That healing has lead to this wonderful journey of creating this whole series of books.

When I started the Are You Happy series I had never imagined I would write not one but four books to share not only my path to success but to help those around me.

Being a teacher and mentor comes naturally to me as does the desire to help others. Yet I understand that can not help everyone, nor will everyone be ready to hear the words contained in these books. It's up to **you** to do the work.

Tools can be given to you but it up to you to use them. It Is up to you and you alone to decide if you are truly happy.

So I ask the question now of you that was asked of me: **What is holding you back?**

Finding the CEO in YOU

Part I
Emerging Effectiveness

Finding the CEO in YOU

Chapter 1: The Basics of Effectiveness

People are facing different challenges in their daily lives. They need to come up with good results to prove themselves or to somebody else that they are worthy of doing so. Basically, these tasks are evaluated according to their degree of effectiveness and efficiency. Whether you are in a business owner, an employee, or an ordinary person at home, it is highly essential to management effectiveness well.

The overall success of what you are currently doing depends how you will get things done right. For this reason, you need to learn what it is all about and how it can totally affect your personality and the things around you.

Bear in mind that the final outcome of what you had done will reflect to you as a person. Thus, you must think and follow what is right naturally. If you want to improve your perception about effectiveness, continue reading and put into your mind and heart all the information you are going to learn.

What is Effectiveness?

Effectiveness refers to the degree in which objectives have been obtained and the extent which target problems have been resolved. It is distinguished with no reference to cost. Effectiveness also means "doing the right thing while efficiency is about "doing such thing right". Another definition that may be incorporated with this word is the ability of intervention to perform more good things than harm for target population in the real world situation.

Personal effectiveness is not all about reaching your goals for you can do it in a time consuming, sloppy, or wasteful way. It implies that you have to start making use of time practically as well as the rest of personal resources. This is how you achieve goals efficiently, such as investment, and get the best return.

Effective individuals are more than those persons who obtain what they exactly want. These people have 2 qualities: They are making the best use of resources and they have been skilled at reaching their goals. Regardless of your main purpose in life, being effective indicates a good combination of skilled execution and efficiency.

People have been personally effective in distinct ways. This is due to the fact that everybody has various values, priorities, and goals in life. For instance, skilled communicators are effective in various ways according to what they wish to achieve. Some individuals who wish to entertain others should have an exceptional sense of humor. Once they impressed a broad audience, then they posses incredible presentation skills. On the other hand, the coach has to become a good listener and communicate sensitively.

Key Themes of Effectiveness

Reliable – consistent, predictable, supports "single truth source", self- correcting

Appropriate – optimizes support and supports for business purposes

Elegant – simplicity, self adapting, clarity, consistency for various human factors

Integrated – supports, creates, and optimizes synergy in the entire systems

Efficient –minimizes resource wastage and optimizes resource use

Effectiveness takes place when all things support everything else. When talking about business, many organizations are focused on giving exerting more efforts for efficiency. Efficiency is just a dimension of the entire effectiveness. To achieve exceptional results, all elements should be managed properly, fairly and consistently.

~Thoughts~

_____
_____
_____
_____
_____
_____
_____
_____
_____
_____
_____
_____
_____
_____
_____
_____
_____

Finding the CEO in YOU

Chapter 2:
Be Proactive

As part of obtaining effectiveness as a person, you have to understand how to be proactive. Being proactive is about taking responsibility when it comes to your actions and life than simply watching how such things happen and pass by. It actually takes time because you need to consider the available options. You need to learn to weigh alternatives wisely and make an informed decision to reach your goals in life. The "reactive" behavior has been influenced by outside forces and environmental factors.

An individual's proactive behavior or pro-activity refers to change-oriented, self-initiated and anticipatory behavior in a particular situation, such as in a workplace. Proactive behavior includes acting on a future situation in advance than simply reacting. This means taking control of things and making them happen than waiting for things to happen or adjusting to such situation.

Proactive behavior has been contrasted with some work-related behaviors, like proficiency or adaptivity. Adaptivity refers to change response, while pro-activity refers to change initiation. Pro-activity has not been restricted to additional role performance behavior.

How to be Proactive?

As you face your daily chances, there have been 2 key approaches to take the necessary action. The first one is the reactive approach, and the other one is the proactive approach.

Proactive approach has been an alternative to reactive action-taking. In this approach, you have to determine the tasks (actions) in advanced .These are the tasks you will take in the entire day. However, at times, you need to stay flexible for some unexpected occurrences. Proactive action-taking has been characterized by providing a possible action thought while making decisions consciously.

The truth is that there are more people who use the reactive action-taking approach than a proactive one. Still, it is possible and straightforward to change an approach. This is how to do it:

Faith in Proactive behavior – the first step is having a mental transformation of what you have believed. To be a proactive action- taker, believe that it will work.

Personal Action Plan – PAP has three initial sections which are comprised of ghost actions, minor actions, and major actions. In order to make it simpler, determine 3 main actions you wanted to do within a day. In the mean time, forget about other ghost or minor actions. Take them on the next part of the process.

Focus on Your Action – After identifying the big actions, start by accomplishing one at a time. Stay for a while and take a break for refreshment. Come back and do the next task. Take these steps until you accomplish the other items on the list.

Avoid reactive triggers – it can be difficult not to fall back to your previous behaviors. Give your best to get rid of reactive action taking through avoiding some common factors around you or the previous things you used to do. Focus on the 3 things you have identified. Do not allow anybody else to ruin your day and your mindset.

Be firm – If you were not used to do so, the proactive approach might be quite odd for you, especially when you were previously a reactive action-taker. Have some time in changing your approach. Never fight against yourself and go back to the old ways. The best thing to do is to go back to being proactive and do better continuously.

To be proactive also indicates anticipating problems, giving your best and finding new solutions. On the contrary, being reactive means resolving problems when turned up, performing minimum effort, and disliking changes. Being proactive is having clear thoughts about personal goals and carrying out right actions to make these goals achievable.

Are You Happy

Habit 1: Be Proactive
I Am the Force

> "Our only freedom is the freedom
> to discipline ourselves."
> --- Bernard Baruch

What does proactive mean?
   Being proactive is the opposite of being reactive. It means to take responsibility for your actions.

So what does reactive mean?
   Reactive means to be acted upon and controlled by events and emotions.

When and where do you tend to be the most *reactive*?
_____
_____

Give an example of a *proactive* choice you've made:
_____
_____

Below are various examples of reactive and proactive language. With two different colored markers, determine which phrases are which by highlighting *proactive language* in one color and *reactive language* in another.

- "It's not my fault!"
- "Can we talk about this first?"
- "I will do that right now!"
- "If only..."
- "Who does he think he is anyway?"
- "Leave me alone, you jerk. It's none of your business!"
- "I'm sorry, I didn't mean that."
- "I just can't decide!"
- "That's unfair!"
- "I didn't see it that way, thanks for letting me know."

Listen to you own language. Is it proactive or reactive? List some examples.
_____
_____
_____

Finding the CEO in YOU

Chapter 3: Clarify Your Goals

Goals provide the direction while it helps a person spend his time constructively. Adjust and change your goals regularly. Goals and priorities do change as time passes by.

Thus, it is highly essential to have a keen review of them every monthly. This way, you can assess where you are going and where you've been at this moment.

Actually, there are techniques to use when you want to clarify your present goals. You do not have to prepare many things just to do so. One way is by writing each of your goals down on a sheet of paper.

Separate them into business and personal categories. Ask yourself if each of them is important to you. If one of them is not, remove that sheet of paper and throw it into the trash can. If yes, keep it there.

Techniques

The next thing to do is to ask yourself whether you are willing to do repeated actions to achieve that goal. If no, remove that sheet of paper and discard it. If yes, keep it. Finally, evaluate what you really wish to achieve. Determine how you are going to measure success against that goal and how you can tell if you were able to achieve it. The most critical question is when you want to achieve this goal.

This is a simple activity is also fun and easy to do. It will definitely help you clarify goals not only by being more specific. Do not hesitate to try this action and see how far you can go.

Finding the CEO in YOU

After discovering your potential to clarify your goals in life, you can encourage other people to do the same thing.

After mastering the process of setting your goals and overcome all the obstacles in your efforts, then you can handle various goals. Make sure that your goals are achievable. These goals should be challenging and measurable. See to it that you can immediately tell if you observe progress or not.

Aside from that, you need to have general time allotment while achieving the goal. Remember that it may not always be possible to have good control of event timings. You must be able to identify the general time length in which you will achieve your goal. It is always essential to make clarifications on the things you wish to get.

However, do not forget that it is also crucial to have good understanding of the reasons of the need to attain them. There are 5 main questions you need to answer during the process of learning how to clarify goals in life.

What is my goal?

_____

_____

_____

_____

Why is it crucial for me to achieve it?

_____

_____

_____

_____

Are You Happy

How can obtaining this goal affect my life?

_____
_____
_____
_____

What benefits will I experience when I achieved this goal?

_____
_____
_____
_____

What do I risk losing if I did not obtain my goal?

_____
_____
_____
_____

There have been more available ways to achieve the most effective and best goal setting in life. All you have to do is to make a good choice and informed decisions in all things you do.

Finding the CEO in YOU

Chapter 4: Learn to Put First Things First

You have to be extra careful if you do not have an idea where you are going. This is due to the reason that you may not actually get there. As you reach the time of leaving behind daily stresses and worries of life, you should start defining the successful exit.

Unless you learned setting and prioritizing your exit objectives or goals, you might have many conflicts.

Prioritizing objects helps you pick your whole path. This task is not really easy, however, doing so can provide a frame to proper decision making.

At some points of your life, you might experience waking up one morning knowing that you got a lot of things to do and you do not have an idea where to get started. Most of the time, all things you need to do may seem to be a priority, making it difficult to determine how or where to start.

First Things First!

To make a ball move forward, start somewhere. There are several planning tactics that are helpful enough when it comes to setting your mind on an immediate execution. Even if long term planning and prioritization are also important, the following techniques below will help you experience progress, on a daily micro level basis.

Provide a list – when you wake up every morning, the first thing to do is to take note of the things that are needed to be accomplished within the day. After writing them down, separate such items into non- urgent vs. urgent to distinguish the main priorities for the day.

Value assessment – Complete your tasks and you will get more advantages than others.

Honesty – when your write down the list of your priorities, try to be realistic with your bandwidth. When you set unattainable goals, you will just be disappointed in the end.

Flexibility – to effectively prioritize, you need to deal with those changing priorities. Get them once they come, then decide carefully if they were urgent or not.

Cutting the Cord – For perfectionists, this is actually where they struggle the most. When a particular task is highly essential, it is easy to be caught up. As a result, you spend much time doing that task or project. Acknowledge every time you do this and try to enforce a strict deadline to get rid of getting down a rabbit hole.

Knowing that you have so many things to do every day can definitely make you feel overwhelmed. However, once you start managing them, you can easily prioritize things easier and faster.

What is your list that you need to prioritize?

_____

_____

_____

_____

_____

_____

Are You Happy

Finding the CEO in YOU

Chapter 5: Understand the Win Win Mentality

The world revolving around all the time was established on a premise that human achievement which thrived around and the common thing present in all people is the "Win-win principle". Most cultures have 'win-win' source.

Win-win is just a part of the 6 total human interaction philosophies. Other part of these philosophies include win/lose, win, lose/lose, no deal or win/win, and lose/win. The most suitable model relies on a situation. If relationships have been paramount, this philosophy is just a viable alternative.

5 Dimensions of a Win-Win Model

In competitive situations in which establishing a relationship has not been crucial, win-lose philosophy can be suitable. There are 5 win-win model dimensions which are listed below:

Character

This is the win-win foundation. There should be integrity to build trust in a relationship and define winning when it comes to personal values. The key trait should be abundance mentality where it is present in everybody (scarcity mentality). Abundance mentality comes from the deep personal security and worth inner sense.

Finding the CEO in YOU

Relationships

This is the focus on win-win. Regardless of the type of person you have been dealing with, relationship serves as the key into turning a situation around. When the emotional and trust bank account balances of a relationship are high, there will be a great probability of having a productive and successful interaction.

Performance Agreements

These are also called partnership agreements which provide direction and definition to win-win. They are shifting the production paradigm from vertical (superior to subordinate) going to horizontal (team/partnership). Developing performance agreements has been the central management activity. It allows people manage themselves within the agreement framework.

Reward System

It is the key win-win model element. When an outstanding performance of some people has been rewarded, other members of the team become losers. Instead, try developing team objectives and individual attainable goals to reward.

Process

The process of win-win has 4 main steps:

Figure out the issue of another point of view; focus on the concerns and needs of other parties.

Determine the main concerns and issues involved.

Identify the possible results after making a very acceptable solution.

Distinguish new choices to obtain the results desired.

You can obtain win-win solutions through win-win procedures. Always remember that win-win mentality has not been the personality technique. This is actually the total human interaction paradigm. It came from the characters of maturity, Abundance mentality and integrity. This grows out of great trust relationships. Win-win has been embodied in the agreements in which it effectively manages and clarifies expectations and accomplishments.

Win-win is seeking for mutual benefits present in the human interactions. It means solutions or agreements have been mutually beneficial. This also serves as a belief which is not "my way" or "your way"; instead, it is "better way", "higher way".

Finding the CEO in YOU

Habit 4 think win win

Are You Happy

Across

2. It all begins with you, It is difficult to think win-win if you have not won the _____ victory first.

4. true or false, developing a win-win attitude is easy

7. This is one of the tumor twins, this is healthy when you use it to challenge yourself but becomes negative when you use it to place yourself above others.

9. This attitude is a selfish attitude that gets ahead at the expense of others and doesn't like to see others succeed.

10. Sometimes no matter how hard you try, you won't find a win-win solution. Don't get upset just agree to disagree, this is also called _ ____ (hint: deal or _ ___).

11. This is the win-win foundation. There should be integrity to build trust in a relationship and define winning when it comes to personal values

13. This attitude believes that everyone can win, You care about yourself and others.

Down

1. These are also called _____ which provide direction and definition to win-win. They are shifting the production paradigm from vertical going to horizontal

3. This is the focus on win-win. Regardless of the type of person you have been dealing with, relationship serves as the key into turning a situation around

5. This attitude is a double negative, and is also known as revenge, You become so caught up in making other people fail, that you begin to fail as well.

6. This attitude is also called "the doormat", This person is nice but doesn't stick up for themselves.

8. This is competitions twin, this habit can keep you from reaching your own personal goals, because you are too busy worrying about others

Finding the CEO in YOU

12. The _____ of the win-win spirit is contagious, and helps everyone succeed (hint: something healthy).

Chapter 6: Learn Empathy

The real great leaders should be empathetic. These people have deep understanding on how to be better at empathy and how to do so. To get started, start with the very basic and analyze the important points carefully.

What is Empathy?

Empathy is an art of perceiving the world just like how somebody else perceives it. If you are empathetic, it only means that you are capable of understanding the feeling of a person in a particular moment and at the same time, understand why such people's actions make sense to him or her.

Empathy allows people to communicate their ideas in the way that are sensible to other people. This has been a part of the building block foundation of greater social interaction as well as powerful and obviously stuff. The good news about it is that it has been the part training and a part talent. Depending on your initial ability level, being good at empathy may require less or more work than somebody else. However, regardless of where you start, you can always educate yourself on how to be more empathetic.

Simple Ways to Learn Empathy

Experience Pain - This is not about living a troubled life. However, when this situation happens, do not ignore it and instead, feel what is happening. Focus on those who are helpful and those who are not. Try to figure out what is something empathetic for you.

Reflect and Collect - Listening along with empathy as you needs to get information first about another person. Know how they feel, what is it about, and why they experience that kind of emotion. After doing so, reflect and make a humble guess on 'where they have been'.

Suspend Judgment – remember that empathy has not been an opinion. Opinions may be required only at certain point. Begin with connection and understanding.

Working on Relevant EQ Skills – examples include understanding non-verbals, listening, thinking or questioning for the perspectives of another person.

Practice – approach certain situations along with deliberate focus when it comes to listening deeply, understanding reflecting back, and connecting.

The way of expressing empathy has been teachable and the indications of looking for in other people are also teachable. The way to feel other people's needs is also teachable. The ultimate thing that cannot be taught is the "desire" of doing it.

Are You Happy

Empathy

```
C I G N E B W M C O N D O L E N C E A Y H Q H T
W H L B L J V G T Y S U D Y S U M X D W T C R N
E J A P Z Z A L Y Y H X H V B D E O H V Y I S E
A W H R H C B C W F K T L X A N X E H P J K P M
O W S C I T C C F X Q K A I D N M V N H S S D R
S Z O O P T D N J Y E C S P D G W M I O T N N E
S Y F N Y S Y W S O N U U Q M J F H F E U T W D
E M T S H Q B T E D X T D M G E K S R S Z C O L
N Y N I T V U X M F R T T V D X O E Y O J D F I
H A E D A S C K P P G Q J D A F O C V R T W E W
S E S E P G O C I R O A E I T T L T N R E E U E
I E S R M A C G O E Y T O H Y U R O E O V N N B
F D E E Y B N F R J A R E P W S U O X W B W D Y
L E N A S Q H H J S A A E N H Q K E E C I L E U
E E E T W Q G Y A D R S X D P F T A O X L J R O
S S Q I M Y T T S T Q G P T G N F M M U V F S W
N V J O S I S S E N D N I K U M P Y F V B C T C
Y V X N N Q E D M D E H Q G T A Q P Y S H Q A D
Y H C A U L N L O V I N G F S Y L F L J D N N D
A S M J E E V T Y M Z Z K S F E Z E J J T Q D C
U U L R S Z G U R E N Q I M H E B B Z B B M I X
H K A S E O X U C R U O V B V A P A T H Y C N W
O C R Q F N Z P V C N P W C L W Q T F I B D G E
H V L J F Q Q T K Y X D X S O A P L W F E D U T
```

UNDERSTANDING   SYMPATHY   STEREOTYPES
SORROW   SOFTNESS   SOFTHEARTEDNESS
SELFISHNESS   PITY   MERCY
LOVING   LABELS   KINDNESS
HUMANITY   HELPFUL   EMPATHY
CONSIDEREATION   CONDOLENCE   COMPASSION
CHARITY   CARELESS   BEWILDERMENT
APATHY

Finding the CEO in YOU

Chapter 7
The Benefits of Being a More Effective Person

People get their self-confidence from you when they had seen that you got confidence in yourself. You should know what to think and not to think.

Always think that you can do and you will succeed in your goals in life. This is where the best confidence starts to come out from your mind and heart. Through effectiveness, your knowledge and skill will grow and from these aspects, you will get confidence. Try new things and make your own self- development plans.

Think about your work more than an occupation. Include enthusiasm, attitude and energy in your daily responsibilities. Pay attention to excellence in every little thing you do. Go beyond your minimum effort, safe path and easy way. Work hard and challenge yourself with something new or different.

The Benefits

Career Learning and Development

It does not matter what particular field you are into. What matters most is your continuous development and learning skills. When you realized the real essence of being an effective person, you will learn that you are doing well in your career. Your personal characteristics will reflect on your daily encounter with your workmates, friends, customers, and other people around.

When you are very effective at your work, you can manage your time well, you communicate clearly, and you got a good attitude. An effective worker has been acknowledged as the most productive and most respected in the workplace.

They are usually the first people considered for promotions. If you are aiming to be recognized as one, then you should strive to achieve effectiveness in all things you do. Once you achieved these things, you will realize that it is worthy to improve your skills in this concept.

Communication Skills

Recall how often you communicate daily. You attend meetings, give presentations, write emails, make calls, talk to clients, and more. Almost all day, you are communicating and connecting with different people around you. That is why excellent communication skills became highly essential especially when the goal is to become more effective at work.

Fortunately, once you start to familiarize your daily routine and apply the necessary solutions, you do not have to worry about other significant aspects.

Having a good communication skill will naturally come out to you as you realize that there is effectiveness in what you do. For this reason, you need to get started in active listening skill development.

It means that you make concerted effort in order to understand and hear what other persons want to tell you. When you already developed good communication and listening skills, you will no longer get easily distracted by different barriers around you.

Productivity and Time Management

Are You Happy

The most important thing you need to do to be an effective person at work is by learning time management perfectly. Without managing your time, your days may seem like to have a race daily with phone calls, emails, projects, and other daily tasks you need to prioritize.

Time management and productivity are the two important factors which every person should learn. They are also the keys to a significant and worth living life that is free from stress and worries.

Other benefits that can be received from being a more effective person include the ability to think logically and clearly. Not all people are capable of thinking logically.

However, it can still be developed and acquired to achieve effectiveness. Another possible advantage is the ability to present ideas and structure thoughts effectively and cohesively. As part of the increased confidence level in conducting yourself with external and internal people, you can obtain set of behaviors which have been beneficial at different aspects.

These are only some of the great things that being an effective person can give you. When you know what to do, there is no reason that you can never be highly effective in your daily tasks. You should always take a look at the good side of doing such thing to perceive things well.

~Thoughts~

Finding the CEO in YOU

Chapter 8: Staying Motivated to be More Effective

Such people find it quite difficult to manage their time and avoid distractions that come along their way. You probably know what to do; however, you cannot make yourself do it. There have been various strategies developed to have a good control of time. In fact, they are obvious enough such as creating a timetable or "To Do" list. So, why don't you try them?

Getting rid of distractions, learn of saying "no", and setting targets can help you do such thing. At the end of the day, only you will be the responsible for your own time management.

Motivation

Setting Goals and Targets

As you explore the ways to become more effective, you should take the path leading you to think about setting targets and your goals in life. First of all, you need to know how to manage time effectively when studying. This way, you already take responsibility.

Next, think about the main reasons why it is a good idea to do such action and where it will end up.

Identify your goals as well as the reward you want to obtain in the near future. It will help you get motivated to become committed in studying or working now.

Finding the CEO in YOU

To know what your targets and goals are, you can make a table divided into three columns. On the first column, try to list your long term goals. On the second column, write about the things to do to fulfill them (medium term goals).

On the last column, write your short term goals to achieve. You can post it on the wall or inside the door of your wardrobe. Mark each goal as you complete them.

Dealing with Distractions

It may be quite difficult to shift your attention to the thing you do when there are many different things that make unpleasant noises or get your attention distractedly. However, if you only make yourself be aware of such things that can get you out of focus, you have to think about ways to manage them.

You will never feel motivated when you think that you always do a particular task. Look for times not to work or study. Try setting an alarm in which you could look for a leisure period to change mode.

Put things in a silent mode so that you will never be distracted.

Value yourself as well as your studies or work. Bear in mind that you only have a very short time to do something. Thus, ensure that it will be done right.

If you want to mix work or studies with other commitments, you cannot really say no to them.

You deserve giving yourself enough time to show your best.

After learning about simple ways and techniques to stay motivated in all things you do, you will be able to set your principles and develop personal management skill. These will help you view a life that is capable of growing in personal effectiveness and confidence.

Are You Happy

Goal phase:

- What is a goal you want to focus on?

___

- When you are successful with this goal, what will it look like?

___

- What makes this goal important to you?

___

- How does this goal fit into your vision?

Finding the CEO in YOU

_____
_____
_____

- When you reach your desired outcome, how would you like to feel?

_____
_____
_____

- What type of change would make your life even better?

_____
_____
_____

Options phase:

- What is some way your goal could be accomplished?

_____
_____

Are You Happy

- Tell me about a time you accomplished something similar?

- What ways have you seen others approach such a task?

- What action can you take to achieve your goal?

Finding the CEO in YOU

- If you choose not to take some of the actions, what will be the impact?

___
___
___

Obstacles phase:

- What could get in the way of you moving forward with pursuing your goal?

___
___
___

- What external challenges might interfere?

___
___
___

- What internal challenges might get in the way?

___

Are You Happy

_____
_____
_____

- Who can you get support from?

_____
_____
_____

Do phase:

- What strategies are you willing to employ to reach your objective?

_____
_____
_____

- What specifically are you going to do, and when?

_____
_____
_____

Finding the CEO in YOU

- How will you know you're making progress?

_____
_____
_____

- What is the most immediate action you can take, and when?

_____
_____
_____

- How long will it take, and when will you complete it?

_____
_____
_____

Chapter 9: Staying on Track

Motivation starts within you. You may get inspired by those achievements obtained by other people. However, when you go far beyond life, then you will also be determined and charged to reach your goals. Take note of the following tips below on how to get motivated and stay on track with your work, study, and life. These will also keep you going at a top speed to become successful in your career.

Staying On Track

Confidence

When you do not believe in your potentials, nobody else would dare also. People have something in which they are definitely good at. Your faith to yourself is very crucial since it is the way you can try working on the niche skills. Forget about your fear of being a loser in the end of your journey.

Bear in mind that what does not kill you can make you even stronger.

Clarity

It is quite hard to stay on focus when it comes to undefined and fuzzy goals. Try asking for measurable and defined tasks and objectives. Have the initiative to work with the right people if necessary. This way, you will have a clarity regarding your definite roles. Self-motivated persons are working best along with their clearly defined life objectives.

Work Independently

Nothing can work better as the motivation power shot compared to the knowledge that you are excellent in what you are doing. Determine your weaknesses and get rid of them all the way. If you want to get familiar with your tasks, study about them carefully. Remember that there are many available methods that you can use to learn something about them. All you have to do is to look around and be a keen observer all the time.

Positively Take Criticisms

Even if other persons do not have intentions, turn those negative criticisms into positive driving forces. Always bear in mind that failure is just a mind state. When you think of being successful, you will. Think positive. This way, you can route frustration to a positive energy needed to work hard. It serves like magic.

Accept Challenges

When your present job does not motivate you, there is no need to worry. Try to become open for new things if a present role gets boring to pursue another day more. Talk to the experts to help you redefine roles to optimize your abilities.

Persistence

Many things do not really work out at the very first time. It only implies that you should try harder. See to it that your heart is set on your important goals and life progress. Never waste your energy on such peripheral things and save extra efforts for useful things.

Be with Successful People

Stay and talk with confident persons who have been driven on life. Continue reading books that can make you optimistic. Do not forget to meet and deal with successful persons and emulate them.

Who are the successful people that you look up to?

_____
_____
_____
_____
_____
_____
_____
_____
_____

Why do you look up to them?

_____
_____
_____
_____

Finding the CEO in YOU

Chapter 10: Making Resolutions for Being an Effective Person

Resolutions are mostly acknowledged when New Year is coming. People think that it is the only time when they have to make intentions throughout the coming year. The truth is that making a resolution should be a part of your daily life encounter. The fact that many people have their own resolutions in life, most of them cannot fulfill them throughout the year.

There can be challenging resolutions you need to commit and make them a reality. However, when you implement them in your life accordingly, you will understand why you are doing such things. There is actually an easy and fun way to start creating an ideal life along with a little effort. This is called "intention".

Intention

Intention is identifying what you really want in life and directing actions to an outcome. Of course, you want to have a harmonious and peaceful life all the way. Or, you might also crave for discovery and adventure. You have the chance to make intentions for a particular situation or as a whole. You may also create trust and connection with the person you love.

Creating these intentions can take a very short period of time. However, this can be an extremely powerful tool for setting a resolution in motion. You do not have to force yourself just to follow a self-improvement plan or get worried how you are going to accomplish different things. Creating good intentions can remove the worry and effort from this process.

Finding the CEO in YOU

It is definitely difficult to become effective especially if you are not confident. To maintain and establish strong confidence, it is highly essential to say and think of positive things about yourself. Recall your best qualities, thing you had done for other people, and things you already achieved in life.

Forget about worries if you do not have long term goals. In fact, there are only a few people who do so. As you obtain and try more new things, continue pushing yourself out of the comfort zone. Establish effective relationships. Always remember that positive relationship has been the crucial key to reach success. Everybody needs to like and trust you in order to deal with your tasks productively. However, if you really want to get their trust, you have to do and show that you deserve one as well. Be an effective person at your best. Live an inspiring life.

Part 2
Become the best Version of Yourself

Finding the CEO in YOU

Are You Happy

From the time we are born, many will be educated to be a version of themselves that please others. Whether it comes from the way you were raised or how you were taught in school, we often learn to put a mask on and be an actor in our life.

Unfortunately, that behavior will not lead you to be happy and live a fulfilling life. You can discover the best version of yourself and transform your life so that you are no longer an actor but rather the CEO of your life. You can **CHOOSE** to live the life that was made for you or **CHOOSE** the destiny that you deserve.

In this section, you will have to commit to exploring yourself, try to be aware of your behaviors, and be honest with yourself. This book is for **you**, and noone other than yourself can know who you are.

With commitment, vulnerability, and curiosity, you will be able to be the best version of yourself and put away the mask that you've to wear for much too long. Are you ready to claim your power?

Then let's start to explore your current life and see how much you are currently your true self!

"The power you have is to be the best version of yourself you can be sothat you can create a better world."
Ashley Rickards

Finding the CEO in YOU

CHAPTER II
BEING YOURSELF

The best version of yourself is being true to yourself, but what does this mean? It is sometimes easier to explain something by identifying what it isn't. That said, here's a list of what is not being the best version of yourself:

- Being true to yourself is not about pleasing others;
- Being true to yourself is not about hurting others;
- Being true to yourself is not about doing things you dislike;
- Being true to yourself is not about forcing yourself to do something;
- Being true to yourself is not about being hard on yourself;
- Being true to yourself is not about judging others and comparing yourself;
- Being true to yourself is not about being a victim of your surroundings;
- Being true to yourself is not about acting in a way that will attract more fans on social media.

Being true to yourself means that you behave and communicate in complete integrity with your belief, values, and, most of all, with what feels right in your heart. When there is an alignment with your inner self (emotions, states, and desires) and outer self (behaviors, communication, and relationships), you are the best version of yourself.

Assessing Yourself

Have you ever felt like your behavior and the way that you held yourself varied depending on who is around you and where you are?

We tend to play a different role when we are with individuals that we want to please or want to make sure that they like us. For example, you might behave in a completely different way if you are at work or with people you just met and want to be friends with them. We tend to be ourselves when we are at home or with childhood friends. That is when we let our guards down and become more vulnerable and less worried about how others might perceive us.

Business, Career and Professional World		
	YES	NO
Are you satisfied with your work?		
Do you get along with your colleagues?		
Do you know what you want to do for work?		
Are you comfortable with your knowledge and skills?		

Are You Happy

	YES	NO
Do you feel you are contributing to the world in a way that fulfills you?		
Are you happy in your career?		
Given the opportunity to change work, would you still stay in your job?		
TOTAL:		

Love and Romantic Relationship		
	YES	NO
Are you experiencing happiness in love?		
Do you feel like you can be yourself in a love relationship?		
Do you feel loved for who you truly are?		

The following questions will help you identify which area of your life you arethe best version of yourself. The answer is yes or no, pick the answer the closest to how you feel (mostly yes or mostly no).

Do you feel your partner knows you very well?		
Are your needs mostly met in your love relationship?		
Is it easy for you to understand your partner?		
Are you healthily independent in your love relationship?		
TOTAL:		
Family		
	YES	NO

Finding the CEO in YOU

	S	O
Are you close to your family?		
Do you feel like you have a connection with your family?		
Can you be yourself around your family?		
Do you mostly experience positive emotions around your family?		
Is being with your family where you feel like you are truly yourself?		
Do you feel supported by your family?		
Can you count on your family when you need help?		
TOTAL:		

Friends

	YES	NO
Do you have a close bond with your friends?		
Do you trust your friends?		
Would you say that the level of "give and take" in your friendship is balanced between you and them?		
Do you feel like you can be yourself with all your friends?		
Do you have healthy boundaries with your friends?		
Do you feel comfortable saying "no" to your friends?		
Are you honest with your friends?		
TOTAL:		

Acquaintances and Neighbors

	YES	NO
Are you honest with people you meet for the first time?		
Do you stay true to yourself when you meet new people? (Meaning you don't change your demeanor.)		

Are You Happy

Are you honest with yourself when you meet someone new that you don't like? (Meaning you don't try to convince yourself that you need to give them a chance.)		
Are you the type of person that will say "no" to an offer to go out if you don't feel like hanging out with that person?		
When you meet someone, do you immediately know if you will get along with them or not?		
Are you able to distance yourself from a person when you are not interested in their friendship?		
Are you comfortable expressing your thoughts with unfamiliar people?		
TOTAL:		

Self

Finding the CEO in YOU

	YES	NO
Are you comfortable in your own skin?		
Do you appreciate your physical body?		
Would you say you have healthy self-talk?		
Are you comfortable with compliments from others?		
Is it easy for you to accept help from others?		
Do you appreciate spending time by yourself?		
Could you list ten qualities about yourself right now?		
TOTAL:		
Compile all the "yes" and "no" from each section. TOTAL:		

Are You Happy

The more "yes" you have, the easier it is for you to be yourself. The goal isto be your true self in all spheres of your life. Based on that quick survey, which area of your life has more "NO"? Keep that in mind; we hope that bythe end of reading this book, you are more comfortable being yourself in that area of your life.

"Every decision you make reflects your evaluation of who you are."Marianne Williamson

~Thoughts~

_____
_____
_____
_____
_____
_____
_____
_____
_____
_____
_____
_____
_____
_____
_____

Finding the CEO in YOU

CHAPTER 12
PROJECTING YOURSELF

Some of the questions in the previous chapter might not make sense to you. For example, we asked if you are "the type of person that will say 'no' to an offer to go out if you don't feel like hanging out with that person." If it is hard for you to say "no" to others and instead of saying "no," you use "white lies," which means that you are also able to tell yourself "white lies." Being dishonest is one of the most common mistakes we make in life that keeps the best version of ourselves at bay.

It takes a long time to realize that the external world is a projection of what is happening internally. Since the external world is a pure reflection of us, it can give us a lot of information about ourselves when we take the time to observe and be aware.

For example, if you hate your job, it could be a sign that you technically don't recognize your skills and abilities. That you are unable to clearly see what you are capable of and therefore settle for jobs that you dislike. It's almost like you are creating your own misery.

Take a moment to list some of the things that you dislike in your environment. That could be the way that your romantic partner treats you, the way that your family makes you feel about yourself or your professional life.

If I could change something about my life, it would be the following:

_____
_____
_____
_____
_____
_____
_____
_____
_____

Now that you've listed a few things you would like to change about your life. Let's reflect on what this means regarding yourself.

Here are a few examples of what could potentially be the projection.

External Projection	Internal Reality
My romantic partner doesn't give me enough attention.	I am struggling to provide myself with love and care.

Are You Happy

My friends don't listen to me or don't want to hear from me; it's always about them.	I tend to forget about my needs and always try to please others. I have a hard time putting myself as a priority.
I'm still stuck doing stuff that I don't like. It seems to always be like that. Why can't others do the things I like?	I am unable to say "no" and have not created healthy boundaries with others. I am not able to respect myself.
I've always hated my jobs and can't seem to find what I want to do in my career.	I am unable to see my skills and abilities. I tend to be hard on myself. I'm never good enough.

When I'm on social media, I want people to like my post. I can take 100s of pictures before I get to the perfect one to share on my social media.	I perceive myself as not enough, and I feel I need to be perfect to be loved. I don't accept myself for who I am. I need the approval of others to like myself.

Finding the CEO in YOU

| Every romantic partner I had, I did everything they wanted and always tried to please them, but they never gave the same amount of effort in the relationship. Why is it that I can't get what I offer? | I believe that I cannot be loved for myself. Therefore, I have to be another person to be liked. I have to act in a certain way to receive love. |

Now, your turn to dig deep and find what your external world is telling you about your internal reality:

External Projection	Internal Reality

Are You Happy

What have you learned about yourself in that activity? Are there aspects of you that you want to work on? Are there some projections that you would like to address and end the cycle in your life?

Finding the CEO in YOU

In the next chapter, we will look at things that make you reactive. Reactivity is often another aspect that needs our awareness. When we learn our triggers, we learn about our true selves and what needs to heal within to be the best version of ourselves.

> *"You don't see the world as it is, you see it according to who you are."* Stephen Covey

~Thoughts~

_____
_____
_____
_____
_____
_____
_____
_____
_____
_____
_____
_____
_____
_____
_____
_____
_____
_____

CHAPTER 13
LEARNING YOUR TRIGGERS

Are there some subjects that you avoid discussing with others because you know you will be angry or frustrated? Do you sometimes find yourself easily offended by others? Learning your triggers will help you to move from being reactive to being at peace with what others think when it is different from your opinion.

When we are triggered by something external to us, we tend to blame others for what we are experiencing. Blaming others for our state of mind and situation is living a victim mindset. The faster you can learn to stop reacting to others; the faster your mindset will shift to be more in alignment with your true self.

First, you have to accept that the only things you can change in this world are your behavior, your mindset, and your communication style. As you probably know by now, you have no control over other people's behavior or mind. Make a decision now that you will no longer blame your problems on external factors.

Second, learn to be aware of your behavior and thoughts, especially when you go in that space of blaming others or reacting to what they do or say. Start by making a list of what you feel trigger you.

Finding the CEO in YOU

Some examples could be politics, injustice, self-centered people, incompetence, etc. Try to be as specific as possible by using an example toexplain the trigger.

I tend to react emotionally to the following:

_____
_____
_____
_____
_____
_____
_____
_____
_____

Now make a plan to react differently in the future when those situations orsubjects arise. How will you better handle your emotions in these situations?

_____
_____
_____
_____
_____

Are You Happy

_____
_____
_____
_____

Another approach to this would be to try to understand why you get so reactive to those situations or subjects. Here are a few examples and what it could mean for a person.

Trigger	Internal Reality
I get so offended when people accuse me of being selfish or self-centered.	I tend to feel like others have it better than me. Therefore, I feel like I don't get what I deserve, and when I focus on my needs, it's because I want what others have.
I get so annoyed when someone talks about women's rights; I just can't stand it.	I feel like it's always been about a woman in my life. When are we going to realize that I am important too, and I deserve what others also deserve?

Finding the CEO in YOU

My partner tells me that I don't give him enough attention and that he feels lonely when we are together.	That makes me so angry because I need my time alone too and he doesn't give me any space, we are always together. I try to ignore him and have my space, but that doesn't work either.
I can't talk about politics; the current situation makes me so mad.	The current political situation is bringing up some deep wounds from past experiences I haven't dealt with in my life.

Now your turn, what triggers you, and when you explore this more profoundly, what does it say about your internal reality?

Trigger	Internal Reality

Are You Happy

Being the best version of yourself means that you are taming the shadows that have been following you, sometimes for years. It's not always easy, butwhen you face your dark side, you bring it to light and immediately allow yourself to shine brighter than ever! It gives you the space to heal deep wounds.

Taking responsibility for your own happiness starts by recognizing your responsibility in your life and stop giving your powers to others. When you blame others, you do not own your responsibility in your life. For example, ifyou continuously blame external factors for the life that you live, you are giving up your powers and will to others. You are allowing others to dictate your behavior and mindset.

By doing so, you are entirely detaching yourself from yourself and merely becoming a pion in life. If you want to be yourself, you have to take ownership of your life. Start by being aware when you blame others for thesituation you are in and shift your mindset to solution finding and own the solution that will get you out of a difficult situation. It's time for you to take back your powers and choose to live the life that you want! When you can maintain a healthy mindset and break the bad habit of reacting to anything,you become more at peace within and better apt to be your best self.

In the next chapter, we will explore your limiting beliefs and how you cantransform them to be more empowering. Those limiting beliefs are often connected to deep wounds from the past that we carry with us for years.

> *"The feeling of being offended is a warning indicator that is showing youwhere to look within yourself for unresolved issues."*
> *Bryant McGill*

CHAPTER 14
KNOCKING DOWN YOUR BARRIERS

There are plenty of reasons why a person would not want to be themselvesfully. According to the Physician and Psychiatrist Dr. John Pierrakos, there are main experiences that create barriers to be our true selves. These barriers are five wounds, were popularized by the famous French author, Lise Bourbeau. Those wounds are abandonment, rejection, injustice, humiliation, and betrayal.

Let's start with a quick assessment that will help you determine which wounds are the most significant barriers to your growth and expression ofyour true self.

	YES	NO
Do you feel like a victim regularly? (A)		
As a child, did you ever feel that you were not wanted? (R)		
Do you lack self-confidence? (A, R, H, I)		
Do you regularly seek solitude? (R)		
Do you do the tasks slowly? (H)		

Finding the CEO in YOU

Do you find it difficult to ask for help? (I)		
Do you think you're stable and very responsible? (B)		
Do you want to be important in life? (B)		
Do you regularly doubt your choices? (I)		
Do you like acting? (B)		
Do you always need a presence around you? (A)		
Do you feel the need to help others all the time? (A, H, B)		
Are you regularly convinced you are right? Do you try to convince others? (B)		
Are you demanding on yourself? (B, I)		
Do you like everything to be in order around you? (B, I)		
Do you generally distrust others? (R, B, I)		
Do you take care of other people's problems before you take care of your own? Do you take care of others moreeasily than yourself? (H)		
Do you often blame yourself; do you regularly feel guilty? (R, A, H, I)		
Do you regularly have breathing problems? (R, A, H)		
Do you often have low blood sugar? Do you have diabetes? (R, A, H)		
Do you often have body tensions? (B, I)		

Are You Happy

Are you hypersensitive to being dirty (take a few showers a day, hate having hands dirty, etc.)? (H)		
Do you easily give up a project, a goal along the way? (R, A)		
Are you impatient, refusing the slowness of others? (B, I)		
Are you bulimic? Or do you struggle with an eating disorder? (H)		
Do you stress or get nervous before you speak? (R, I)		
Do you feel anxious before you go on a trip, facing a change in your life? (A)		
Do you use drugs or alcohol all the time? (R, A, H)		

SCORING				
CALCULATE ALL THE YES FOR EACH LETTER				
(R) REJECTION	(I) INJUSTICE	(H) HUMILIATION	(A) ABANDONMENT	(B) BETRAYAL
/10	/10	/10	/10	/10

Now that you can see which wound has the most yes out of 10. Let's explore each one of those obstacles in your life and help you understandthose deep wounds. Even if you didn't score high on some wounds, readthe content because you might still relate with some of the information provided below.

Rejection

Rejection is a profound wound because the one who suffers from it feels rejected in his being and especially in his right to exist. Therefore, it is practically impossible to be yourself when you wear that wound. It is not unusual for people who feel rejected to have a fleeing physique, that is to say, a body or a part of the body that seems to want to disappear or become very small. As if the receding person wanted to go unnoticed for fear of being rejected.

In terms of behavior, they often doubt their right to exist. They seek solitudebecause if they receive a lot of attention, they would be afraid of not knowing what to do. They can be fleeing, which is why they prefer not to get attached to material things because they would prevent them from running away. They often wonder what they are doing on this planet and finds it hard to believe that they could be happy here and bring something to this world.

They don't know what to do with themselves when they get too much attention. In relationships with others, they are constantly finding ways to seek love from the parent of the same sex and will reject themselves from aperson of the other sex, often feeling guilty when they face rejection. It is not unusual for them to live in ambivalence; when they are accepted, they won't believe it and often create a self-sabotaging situation so that othersreject them. Their biggest fear is panic and anxiety because that often arises in them when they are rejected.

Are You Happy

Injustice

The wound related to injustice is intimately linked to the wound of rejection. While rejection touches deeply the "being," the wound of injustice touches on having and doing. People who have that wound often has a body rigid, and as perfect as possible. They have a well-proportioned body; Rigid movements; Stiff neck; and very proud.

They are usually lively persons with dynamic movements, but who is rigid and lacks flexibility. Often a perfectionist and envious. These persons tend to cut themselves off from their feelings and often cross their arms. They tryto be perfect and justifies themselves a lot. They find it difficult to admit thatthey have problems. They often doubt their choices. They like order and tend to control themselves by demanding a lot from each other. They can be angry and cold and has difficulty showing affection. They don't want to be late but will often be delayed because they take a long time to prepare.

It is often difficult for people with the injustice wound to accept compliments, help, or gifts from others because they feel in debt toward theperson after. Their biggest fear is when others are cold toward them because that awakens the unfairness but is also a reflection of their shadow.

Humiliation

This wound is mostly related to the physical aspect of having and doing. Most individuals with the humiliation wound have a larger and round body, round face, with a broad and rounded neck.

They are often ashamed of themselves and others or afraid to shame others. They think they are dirty or unclean. They don't want to recognize and assume their sensuality and their love of the pleasures associated with the senses. That is why they often compensate and reward themselves with food. And they gain weight quickly to give themselves a reason not to enjoy their senses. They are also afraid of being "punished" if they enjoy life too much. So, they ignore their freedom by putting the needs of others before their own, so that they stop enjoying life.

Most individuals with the humiliation wound want to do everything for others. In reality, they want to create constraints and obligations for themselves to stop enjoying their freedom and life. This lack of enjoyment reinforces the feeling of being abused and humiliated. And in the same way, they tend to demean and humiliate others by making them feel that they cannot do it alone without them. They are often inclined to blame themselves for everything and even take the blame for others. Their biggest fear is their freedom; they are afraid to lose the ability to be themselves when humiliated by others.

Are You Happy

Abandonment

The wound experienced in the case of abandonment is the second deepestafter that of rejection because they both affect the being at a profound level.

Most people with the abandonment wound lack tonus. Their body is usuallylong and slender with a back that becomes rounded and sagging. As if the spine and muscles were not able to keep the body upright. Their body seems to need help to hold on.

Those who suffer from abandonment do not feel emotionally nourished enough. They need constant help and support. They think that they cannotdo anything on their own and regularly needs someone to support them.
They often have ups and downs: for a while, they are happy, and everything is fine, and suddenly, they feel unhappy and sad. They tend to dramatize a lot: the smallest little incident takes on gigantic proportions. In a group, they like to talk about themselves and often brings everything backto them.

Besides, they usually seek the opinion or approval of others before makingdecisions. They can't make up their mind, or they doubt their choice when they don't feel supported by someone else. And when they do something for someone, they do it with the expectation of a return of affection. Their problems give them the gift of attention, and this prevents them from beingabandoned. The more a person acts like a victim, the more his or her abandonment wound increases. Their greatest fear is loneliness since it is directly connected to that feeling of being abandoned.

Betrayal (or Treason)

The wound of betrayal is intimately related to the wound of abandonment).While abandonment is about being, the wound of betrayal is about having and doing.

Their body often exhibits strength and power. In men: shoulders wider thanthe lower body. In women: lower body larger than the shoulders (pear- shaped body). The higher the asymmetry between the upper and lower body, the greater the betrayal wound.

Very uncompromising, they want to show others what they are capable of.They often interrupt and respond before a person is finished. When thingsdon't go fast enough to their liking, they become angry. They consider themselves hard-working and responsible: they struggle with laziness.

They hate not being trusted and do not always keep their commitments andpromises or forces themselves to keep them. They tend to be impatient and intolerant. They confide with difficulty and do not show their vulnerability.

People with a betrayal wound have great difficulty accepting the cowardiceof others. They also have trouble delegating tasks while trusting others.

Are You Happy

Among the five wounds, the betrayal wounded is the one who has the most expectations towards others because he likes to foresee and control everything. Unlike abandonment wounded who has expectations of others because they want to be loved and supported in their abandonment injury, the expectations of the betrayal wounded are to check that others do what they need to do well to verify if they can trust them.

They firmly state what they believe and expect others to agree with their beliefs. They tend to state their point of view categorically and seeks to convince others at all costs. They think that when someone understands them, they agree with them, which unfortunately is not always the case. Their biggest fears are disengagement, separation, dissociation, and denial, which are often experienced in a situation of betrayal.

It is essential to know what your wounds are to identify your limits and what obstacles stop you from being your true self. By being aware of your behaviors and wounds, you are getting to know yourself better and also understanding why you tend to behave in specific ways. Maybe one of your wounds is betrayal, and you get very insecure in your relationship when your partner doesn't live up to your expectations, by knowing that about yourself, you can learn to improve the relationship and how you react to certain situations.

The first step to heal your wounds is to observe yourself when you feel hurt(chapter 10 will help you with that). Then you can move on to accept that you aren't perfect, and it's OK to recognize the hurt. Last is to admit your fear and allow yourself

Finding the CEO in YOU

to move through that fear by being vulnerable and honest with yourself and others.

"Whether you think you can or think you can't. You're right."
Henry Ford

~Thoughts~

_____
_____
_____
_____
_____
_____
_____
_____
_____
_____
_____
_____
_____
_____
_____
_____
_____
_____
_____
_____
_____
_____

CHAPTER 15
CREATE BOUNDARIES

Boundaries are one of the most underused ways to be the best version ofyourself. You must learn to say "no." Saying "no' is probably one of the hardest things you'll ever have to do to ensure you are in integrity with yourself.

Most people are not used to hear "no" or respect "no." To learn to say "no,"you have to explore how you react to people who say "no" to you. Once you are open to others saying "no" to you, start practicing it yourself. Say "no" when you don't feel like doing something or when it doesn't feel right for you.

Another aspect of creating boundaries is how you behave in your friendshipcircle. Be clear about individuals who are supportive and uplift you and stayaway from those who only bring you down, or feed drama. Surround yourself with people who appreciate you for who you truly are. Now it the perfect time to assess your friendships and set boundaries around those who do not fulfill you.

Toxic relationships often feel a more deep-seated need to please others. Ifyou are experiencing a relationship with a person who is mean to you or always makes you feel bad about yourself, knows that you are allowing this. It is OK for you to say "no" to that type of relationship. It doesn't have to be a romantic relationship; it could be with a friend or a coworker.

Finding the CEO in YOU

To have healthy boundaries, you need to know what you value. If you value compassion, but you turn around and start criticizing and gossiping with a friend, you are not in integrity with yourself. Be clear about what you value and then match the behaviors to those values. That way, it will be easier to create boundaries and shift your behavior when it is not aligned with your values and beliefs. Once you are clear with your values, seek them in others, and surround yourself with people who have similar values to you.

Once you can recognize how you feel about the relationship you currently have and are clear about your values, it will be much easier to assert yourself. For example, if you are with a group of friends and one suggests something you are uncomfortable about, you can assert yourself.

Express how you feel and why you don't feel like participating in that idea. The more you will assert yourself, the better you will feel about yourself.

Just be mindful that you are not judging or criticizing others when you assert yourself. Position your thoughts in a way that it's about what you feel and what you don't feel is aligned with your true self.

But most of all, stop trying to please others because it is one of the most limiting behaviors you can have. When you please others, you completely forget your true self and allow others to dictate how you should behave, look, and even talk. This type of behavior is very destructive to the self, and it is pretty much "acting" yourself. You become an actor and live the life that others want you to live in.

Once you learn to let go of pleasing others, you start living your own life. You no longer tailor your experience to the image of others but more to what you want and who you are. By doing so, the people around you will accept you for who you are, and if they don't accept you, they are not meant to be in your life.

Creating boundaries means recognizing that sometimes you do things to please others, and that has to stop if it makes you feel bad about yourself. Pay attention to when you say "yes," and deep down, you don't feel like doing something. Take the courage to stop trying to please others. For example, if somebody asks you to do something for them and you don't feel it's aligned with your needs, just say that it's not a good time for you. You can also say "**no**."

Doing what you want doesn't mean free for all; it means showing compassion toward what lies in your heart and do things that bring you joy, fulfillment, and drive. The more you will do things that bring you joy, the less you will need boundaries; you will surround yourself with people who appreciate you for who you are. You won't need to say "no" because it will be aligned with your true self.

Once you start setting boundaries, you will notice your life-changing, and you will find yourself experiencing more positive moments. A life with boundaries is the perfect environment to be yourself and live your best life.

If you want to be the best version of yourself, you need to learn to say no and create boundaries. By distancing yourself from things that don't align with your authentic self, you are saying no to distraction and hindrance to living your best life.

Finding the CEO in YOU

When you start respecting yourself, you put yourself as the priority. Many people believe it is selfish; meanwhile, when it is done for the right reasons, it serves a bigger purpose. It allows you to have the time, energy, and wellness to be your best self around others.

It will enable you to be present for others and, in return, uplift them too. When you find the courage to create healthy boundaries in your life, you quickly are rewarded with joy, happiness, and a sense of being the best version of yourself.

"Setting boundaries is a way of caring for myself. It doesn't make me mean, selfish, or uncaring (just) because I don't do things your way. I care about me too.
Christine Morgan

Are You Happy

Setting Boundaries

 Personal boundaries are the limits and rules we set for ourselves within relationships. A person with healthy boundaries can say "no" to others when they want to, but they are also comfortable opening themselves up to intimacy and close relationships.

Know Your Boundaries

Boundaries should be based on your values, or the things that are important to you. For example, if you value spending time with family, set firm boundaries about working late.

Your boundaries are yours, and yours alone. Many of your boundaries might align with those who are close to you, but others will be unique.

Know your boundaries *before* entering a situation. This will make it less likely you'll do something you're not comfortable with.

What to Say

You always have the right to say "no". When doing so, express yourself clearly and without ambiguity so there is no doubt about what you want.

"I'm not comfortable with this"	"Please don't do that"	"Not at this time"
"I can't do that for you"	"This doesn't work for me"	"I've decided not to"
"This is not acceptable"	"I'm drawing the line at ___"	"I don't want to do that"

What to Do

Use Confident Body Language
Face the other person, make eye contact, and use a steady tone of voice at an appropriate volume (not too quiet, and not too loud).

Be Respectful
Avoid yelling, using put-downs, or giving the silent treatment. It's okay to be firm, but your message will be better received if you are respectful.

Plan Ahead
Think about what you want to say, and how you will say it, before entering a difficult discussion. This can help you feel more confident about your position.

Compromise
When appropriate, listen and consider the needs of the other person. You never *have* to compromise, but give-and-take is part of any healthy relationship.

Finding the CEO in YOU

1. Know Your Rights

It's impossible to set healthy boundaries if you don't know what your boundaries are. This first exercise will help you to identify them.

Take some time to consider your rights and write them down. Think about different relationships and situations in your life and your rights in each of them.

For example, with your partner, you have the right to express yourself, feel safe physically and emotionally, and express your sexuality as you desire.

At work, your rights may include not being discriminated against or contacted outside of working hours.

With your family, you may feel it's your right to put your needs first before helping others.

Listing your rights is a powerful exercise as it will help you to identify areas of your life where your boundaries are weak and need to be strengthened.

_____

_____

_____

_____

2. Find Your Core Values

We all have different personal values, and they are the foundation of our boundaries, so it's essential to get clear about your values for successful boundary-setting.

In your relationship, your values may include having shared interests or working towards common goals.

At work, your values may include having a healthy work-life balance or a strong company culture.

Your family values may include spending quality time together or even limiting the amount of time spent together.

Write down your ten most important values, then narrow them down to 3 or 4 core values. Keep these values in mind at all times.

This will help you determine what you can accept or tolerate and what you will not accept in any given situation.

3. Establish Your Boundaries

Once you are clear on your core values, it's time to turn them into boundaries.

For each core value, ask yourself the following 3 questions:

1. What will I allow given this value?

2. What will I tolerate given this value?

3. What will I not allow given this value?

Write your answers down for future reference.

4. Communicate Your Boundaries

Communicating your boundaries lets the other person know what your expectations of them are.

Since we all have different boundaries, we all cross the line with one another sometimes.

Usually, it's unintentional, so letting someone know where your boundaries are will help them avoid crossing them in the future.

Using nonviolent communication to establish your boundaries is essential.

Do not approach the conversation from a place of blame as this will most likely lead to conflict.

Instead, take a **problem-solving approach**.

You are simply sharing your boundaries with the other person to inform them of how their actions cross your boundaries.

Share how the other person's actions impact you and explain how this relates to your core values.

For example, you could say your boss: "One of my core values is having a healthy work-life balance so that I can spend time with my family. When you ask me to work overtime without warning, I feel that crosses a boundary and comprises my core value."

This will help them understand what your boundaries are without becoming defensive — which means they will be much more receptive to taking your message on board.

5. Maintain Your Boundaries

Life is messy — especially when it comes to relationships — and people can still cross your boundaries from time to time, even after you have clearly communicated them.

When dealing with crossed boundaries, keep your **core values** at the forefront of your mind and refer to them during the conversation.

For example, you could say to your partner: "I love you and I want our relationship to be successful.

Since cooperation is one of my core values, we need to cooperate in order to succeed.

When you leave the dirty dishes in the sink after I make dinner, I feel you are not cooperating and that makes me sad. How can we cooperate better?"

Finding the CEO in YOU

This is a much more constructive approach that will lead to less conflict and greater harmony and understanding in the relationship.

🎯 Practice

Situation: You invited a friend over for the evening, but now it's getting late. You would like to get ready for bed, but your friend seems unaware of how late it is.

Response:

Situation: A good friend asks you out on a date. You are not interested in being more than friends. You would like to let them down clearly, but gently.

Response:

Are You Happy

Situation: You missed several days of work due to a medical condition. When you get back, a coworker asks what happened. You feel this information is personal, and do not want to share.

Response:

Situation: Your brother asks if you can watch his two young children on Saturday morning. You already have plans.

Response:

Situation: Your coworker is upset about their recent performance review. They start yelling and slamming their fist on their desk. This is making you very uncomfortable.

Response:

Situation: A salesperson comes to your door during dinner. You try to politely show disinterest, but they keep giving their sales pitch. You want to get back to dinner.

Response:

Finding the CEO in YOU

~Thoughts~

CHAPTER 16
INCREASE YOUR SELF-CONFIDENCE AND SELF-ESTEEM

Self-confidence is mostly behavior-based, and it is about knowing what your abilities are while self-esteem is more mind based on how you perceive yourself. Self-esteem and self-confidence are not always positively correlated. For example, you can be good at something and trustyour skills (self-confidence) but still perceive yourself as a loser (self- esteem). First, let's explore self-confidence and assess how your self-confidence is.

Self-Confidence

Self-confidence is about trusting your abilities and also trust your own judgment and decisions. People with low self-confidence will judge themselves by their actions or what they are incapable of doing. When youexperience low self-confidence, you will likely see the gaps in yourself.

Here are some questions that will help you assess your self-confidence(check all that applies to you).

- ❑ I do what is expected of me even when it doesn't necessarily feelright.
- ❑ I often feel sad and discourage about my life.
- ❑ It's hard for me to handle change.

Finding the CEO in YOU

- ❑ When something looks hard, I usually don't even try it.
- ❑ I rarely set goals for myself.
- ❑ I rarely find solutions to my problems.
- ❑ When I receive feedback, I often feel hopeless.
- ❑ Obstacles are failures for me.
- ❑ I can't list five of my qualities right now.
- ❑ I feel like I don't have the abilities, resources, and skills to accomplishyour goals.
- ❑ I rarely take a risk because that often means failure for me.

The more answers you've checked, the more you need to work on yourself-confidence.

One of the easiest ways to work on self-confidence is to assess your level of comfort at accepting compliments from others and correct it. How do youreact when someone gives you a compliment or positive feedback? Most people who struggle with that will show a lower level of self-confidence.

Correcting this is simple: learn to respond with "Thank You." Stop making excuses or reasons for it, and simply say thank you. This will improve yourrelationship with others and, mostly, with yourself. If you can't accept compliments from others, how can you expect to recognize your qualities?Start by showing a different behavior in your external world and the inner world will positively change.

Another way to build self-confidence is to strengthen your self-esteem, which is more the way you perceive yourself.

Improve your perception ofyourself, and you are less likely to see the gaps in your behaviors.

Self-Esteem

Self-esteem is the way we perceive or evaluate our worth and is the ultimate belief we place on ourselves. People with high self-esteem tend to be more comfortable with their true selves and demonstrate a lot moreintegrity.

When we have high self-esteem, we respect our true selves. On the other hand, people with low self-esteem will often stop themselves from doing something or from expressing who they are because they fear that they willnot be accepted and love for who they are.

Our fear of being judged often lead us to behave in a way that is not aligned with what our heart wants because we want to feel accepted andloved by others. To get over this fear, you have to let go of the need for approval from others slowly. You can do so by taking the time to accept yourself first, and then you can express who you are without feeling like others will judge you.

Let's evaluate your level of self-esteem; check all that applies to you.

- ❑ I am comfortable and happy to be myself
- ❑ I recognize my qualities and skills
- ❑ I have a lot of respect for who I am
- ❑ I can be as valuable as any other person
- ❑ I enjoy being myself, as opposed to a persona to please others

- ❏ Failure is not something I see in myself; Instead, I see failures as opportunities for growth
- ❏ I feel that I am worthwhile
- ❏ I can look at myself in the mirror and feel comfortable and loving toward myself
- ❏ I don't expect everyone to like me and that is OK, I don't feel the need to change for them
- ❏ I'm always open for growth and yet, love and accept myself as I am
- ❏ I can be my biggest fan

The more answers you've checked, the higher is your self-esteem. To develop your self-esteem, you can work on the following.

Appreciate Yourself

Appreciating yourself means that you are OK with who you are and enjoy being by yourself. Have the goal of becoming your best friend. Take some time to hang out with yourself once in a while. It will help you build a level of comfort in being by yourself. Add some self-care during those moments; it will help you increase self-respect.

Be Proud of Your Accomplishments

We've all accomplished something in our life. It could be as simple as completing your elementary school or getting that job you applied for.

Whatever it is, take the time to list the things you've accomplished in yourlife, even if it is as simple as making your bed!

Recognize Your Skills

Every one of us is good at something. If it's hard for you to identify those skills, ask someone around you to help list a few abilities that you have. It can be hard skills like carpentry, drawing, or cooking. It could also be a softskill like listening, compassion, or empathy.

Learn to Love Your Body

Learning to love our bodies is probably one of the most significant accomplishments we can make in our life. Some studies show that 40% of men and over 90% of women are unhappy with their bodies. That is almostunreal! Loving your body is about self-talk (which will be covered in chapter 9) but also about self-respect. Be your best friend and treat your body the same way you would treat your child or best friend. Be kind, compassionate, and supportive.

Compassion toward ourselves will often lead to better self-esteem and higher self-confidence. There is also an aspect of connecting with the selfthat becomes important. This is the subject of the next chapter.

"One can only hope the person you love will make you the best version ofyourself."
Mia Maestro

Finding the CEO in YOU

~Thoughts~

CHAPTER 17
CONNECTING WITH YOUR AUTHENTICITY

Authentic people are genuine, real, and mostly, in integrity with themselves. They don't try to be someone they are not or please people they don't know. They, in some ways, know that they are unique but accept that aspect of themselves. For them, being different is not an issue nor something they thrive to be; they are just themselves.

Authentic people also love doing what they enjoy and don't try to copy others' ideas for the sake of being successful. Their success comes from doing what is in their heart, what drives them, as opposed to what inspire others or the majority.

One of the best ways to connect with your authentic self is to stop comparing yourself to others. When you compare yourself to others, you automatically feed a belief that you should be like others, that being yourself is not enough. This limits you from being yourself and making it OK. Most of us often compare ourselves to others because we have that belief that others have it better than us. This can transform into envy or jealousy.

Finding the CEO in YOU

Take a moment to list all the things that make you happy and fulfill a spacein your heart:

_____
_____
_____
_____
_____
_____
_____
_____

Now find ways to do more of that. When you do the things that you love, you are being authentic, you are exposing the best version of yourself, andthat's why it is fulfilling. Another way to reconnect with your true and authentic self is to rediscover your inner child, the one that didn't care about what others thought.

> *"Authenticity is the daily practice of letting go of who we think we'resupposed to be and embracing who we are."*
> *Brené Brown*

CHAPTER 18
RECONNECTING WITH YOUR INNER CHILD

When you reconnect with your inner child, you also heal wounds from thepast (often associated with the five wounds in chapter 4.). The top things you can learn from your inner child are the following:

- There is no such thing as failures, only experiences. The best way to experience life is through play.

- It doesn't matter what others think. If you want to scream, scream; if you want to dance in public, dance in public; if you want to sing when you eat, sing when you eat.

- Love is unconditional. I love my parents no matter what or who they are, from the moment I am born.

- I live in the present moment. When I am hungry, you know it; When I am happy, you know it; When I am calm, you know it. I am not afraid to express how I feel.

- It's easy to forgive others; you just have to show compassion and move on.

Finding the CEO in YOU

Try to be more like your inner child and awaken that aspect of you that youknew when you were young, but somehow, you've disconnected from growing up. Take the time to play again, to make mistakes, forgive and try something else. Don't be afraid to be vulnerable and do what your hear tells you to do, no matter what others may think. Love yourself and others around you learn to love unconditionally once again, show compassion to those around you. And most of all, learn to live in the present moment, stopresisting all those emotions and learn to express them more healthily (and not repress).

> *"The most potent muse*
> *of all is our own inner child."*
> *Stephen Nachmanovitch*

~Thoughts~

_____
_____
_____
_____
_____
_____
_____
_____
_____
_____
_____
_____

CHAPTER 19
TAME YOUR INNER VOICE

Self-talk is one of the most powerful forms of communication because it has the power to lift you up or bring you down in a matter of seconds.

It is often impressive how we can be mean to ourselves. While most of us would never express hate or diminishing words toward our friends and families, yet, we let ourselves be our biggest bully.

The first step is to pay attention to your inner chat. What are the thoughts that cross your mind when you look at yourself in the mirror or when you make a mistake? Be aware that if you practice negative self-talk, this didn't happen overnight, and it will require a lot of practice, awareness, and work to get the habit out of you.

Second, try to identify when you are using a lot of negative self-talk.
Is it when you look at yourself in the mirror?

_____
_____
_____

Finding the CEO in YOU

When you are out with friends or when you are at work?

_____
_____
_____

Once you've identified it, make a new affirmation that will replace your negative self-talk.

For example, if you are always criticizing yourself when you are at the gym (ex: that your hips are too big or your belly is not in enough), make a new phrase in your mind that you will use when you are exercising. It could be that you are proud of yourself for taking the time to take care of you physical body. Be aware of your negative chatter and change it to something more positive.

"Self-talk reflects your innermost feelings."
Asa Don Brown

_____
_____
_____
_____
_____
_____
_____
_____

CHAPTER 20
INCREASE YOUR SELF-AWARENESS

Have you ever been in a public space, and the person next to you express this huge sigh that clearly shows her impatience toward the situation? How did that make you feel? Were you a bit uncomfortable?

That person didn't care about self-awareness. Self-awareness is the ability to recognize your emotional state and find ways to stay in balance. When you practice self-awareness, you are automatically allowing yourself to be abetter version of yourself and not let your emotions take control of you.

Being self-aware simply means that you can observe yourself from a non-judgmental perspective.

When you are self-aware, you can catch yourself in the present momentexperiencing a specific state, reaction, or feeling.

The more you are aware of your emotions, the more you start tounderstand yourself.

For example, you might observe that you tend to be reactive when someone provides you with a suggestion on how to do something different.When you are aware of your emotions, you have a better idea of who you are and how you tend to react in certain situations. It is also the best way to improve yourself on certain aspects that you don't find optimal. You become less driven by drama.

Self-awareness will help you in your daily life with identifying moments when you are living one of the five wounds, or when you are a victim and not aligned with the best version of yourself. Self-awareness will also help you with the following:

- Experience a greater ability to recognize your emotions
- Improve your critical thinking
- Improve your relationships
- Live in the present moment
- Experience more joy and happiness

But the ultimate reward to being self-aware is your ability to recognize when you are not in alignment with your true self. It is the opportunity to be authentic and therefore be in integrity with yourselves. Self-awareness is the key to becoming the best version of yourself.

"Awareness is the greatest agent for change."
Eckart Tolle

Are you Happy

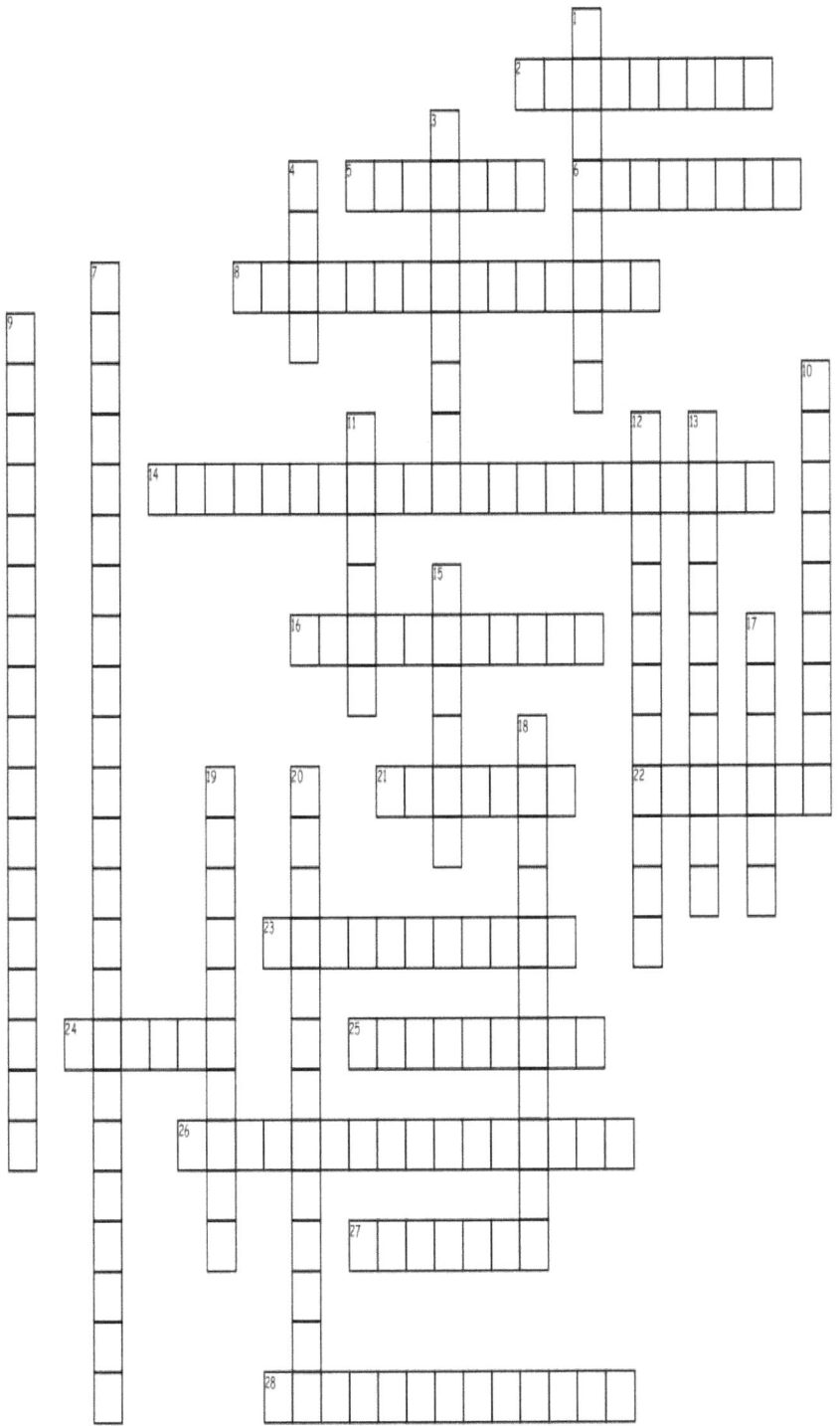

Finding the CEO in You

Across

2. _____ of your personality helps you analyze such a decision
5. Consideration, Especially for others
6. A person's outlook on life usually positive or negative
8. The physical Geographic surroundings and condition of your workplace
14. One of the five facets of emotional intelligence
16. Needs cause _____
21. A person with high emotional self awareness understands the internal process associated with emotional experiences and therefore, has _____ control over them
22. _____ with well developed emotional self awareness are more effective intuitive decision makers
23. When needs aren't satisfied it can cause _____
24. The behaviors that we repeat routinely, and often automatically
25. To become more _____ we should develop an understanding of ourselves in many areas
26. Feedback on your characteristics and behaviors helps your develop your _____
27. A skill that has been developed
28. Knowing your personal characteristics and how your actions affect other people

Down

1, _____ who are highly emotionally self aware are better able to read their "gut feelings" and use them to guide decisions
3. The natural ability or potential for learning new skills
4. You will need to work extra _____ to develop skills for that job
7. Understanding your own feelings what causes them and how they impact your thoughts and actions
9. The environment of the workplace which includes noise, stress, and safety, etc.
10. Self awareness helps you exploit your _____ and cope with your weaknesses

Are you Happy

11. Key areas for self awareness include our personality traits, personal values, _____, emotions and the psychological needs that drive our behaviors

12. Jobs that don't suit your _____ tend to give your more stress than jobs that are more compatible
13. The information vacuum around a leader created when people withhold important information
15. When we focus on our _____ we are more likely to accomplish what we consider most important
17. Self awareness will _____ a skills gap that you want to work on
18. The combination of attitude, values, interests, and behaviors that identify a person
19. It's very difficult to cope with poor results when you don't _____ what causes them
20. Natural method or way one thinks or learns

Being the best version of yourself is not an objective that we can reach overnight. As a human being, we first have to accept that we aren't perfect, and perfection will never be our truth. As you have learned from this book, being the best version of yourself is not about perfection but more about finding your true self.

The true self can only be found when we choose to remove the mask that we've been wearing for a long time. That mask comes with behaviors and wounds that only time and hard work can heal. Don't be afraid to face yourshadows and bring to light the aspect of yourself that needs to heal.

Never forget that human was never meant to be alone and do things on their own. We are social creatures that require a community to thrive. Don'thesitate to seek help from experts or build a support network on encouraging and motivating you to grow.

    Every month, try to redo the assessment that is located in chapter 1 of this section, it willbe a great way to identify if you are getting closer to being the best versionof yourself. That assessment will also help you determine which area still needs more work and why not make a goal out of it! No matter what, you got this and embrace the best version of yourself today!

~Thoughts~

_____
_____
_____
_____
_____
_____
_____
_____
_____
_____
_____
_____
_____
_____

Part 3

Business & Life Transformations

Finding the CEO in You

Chapter 21

Working From Home

If you run a business from home, then it's important to recognize that it's going to mean living a completely different lifestyle from the majority of people you know. Not having a commute in the morning, not spending all day sitting in an office and being able to generally create your own working hours puts you on an entirely different page from most people you'll know.

For the most part, this is a good thing. Being able to set your working hours, to dictate the way you work and when you work and getting to spend time doing something you love can all contribute to a much happier and healthier lifestyle on the whole. In fact, it's a starting point for improving overall health.

At the same time though, this type of lifestyle also brings with it its own challenges. And because very few people live the same lifestyle you do, that means you're going to be somewhat 'on your own' when it comes to finding advice on how to manage this work/life balance.

Well, until you found this book anyway!

Here's the long and the short of it: being self-employed and working from home gives you the freedom to begin your own 'lifestyle design'. This is pretty much the way things are moving and is likely the future of working. Technology is making it possible for us to work remotely in more and more industries and more and more roles. The benefits of this kind of work drastically outweigh the cons – for both the employee and employer – and so the traditional office may soon become a rarity rather than the norm.

That means the emphasis is on increasingly more of us to look after our own health and work/life balance. This book will help you to do just that.

Working From Home: The Possible Health Benefits

As mentioned, when done right, working from home has the potential to lead to incredible health benefits.

Let's look at the facts. Most of the population is overweight, overtired and over-stressed. If you can still remember working in an office, then no doubt you will recall what it felt like to have a full on day in the office, to travel home for an hour on the train/bus or in the car and then to have to cook dinner when you got back.

What did you most often end up doing? You threw something in the microwave and you collapsed in front of the television. And then when your friends called to invite you out, you ignored that and carried on 'vegging out'.

Many of us talk about 'time management' and we say that the reason we don't stick to a training regime/weight loss program is that we don't have the time. This is in fact all wrong. Most of us have plenty of time (otherwise, how did you manage to fit in the entire series of Lost recently?) but what we lack is the energy. Without energy, we don't have will-power. Without will-power, things don't get done and we start to drown in a list of things we need to be doing and become incredibly stressed. Our bodies suffer, our relationships suffer and we don't live life to the fullest.

Working from home can change all that. Working from home means that you can choose to work out in the morning or in the afternoon – you just have to choose the time that you have the most energy. At the same time, it means you can put food on the stove while you're working and watch it simmer.

Working from home means you can sit outside and feel the sun on your face, instead of being cooped up in an office (which is known to contribute to stress and depression). Working from home means that you don't have to commute down busy streets with hundreds of people walking at you during rush hour – this wreaks havoc with your heart rate.

In short, when you work from home you get to choose your priorities and you reduce the stress of working several times over. Now you can put yourself first and that's an incredibly important and valuable thing to be able to do.

The potential health benefits are trans-formative and life-changing. This book will show you how to start working from home if you don't already and how to take maximum advantage of that situation so that you're able to feel your very best and feel the benefits in every other area of your life.

Oh and of course this will have a powerful knock-on effect and impact on your productivity helping you to get more work done and to a much higher quality.

~Thoughts~

_____
_____
_____
_____
_____
_____
_____
_____
_____

Working From Home
The Health Risks

But this book won't just be about capitalizing on the amazing health benefits of working from home. Just as importantly, we'll be looking at the potential health risks that working from home can pose. And make no mistake: there are many.

Think being shouted at by your boss is stressful? How about being shouted at by 10 angry clients? Or 300 angry customers who just downloaded your app?

And here's the difference between working for someone versus working for yourself: when you work for someone else and you have an unproductive day, you still get paid.

When you work for yourself and you have an unproductive day? You get nothing.

Are you Happy

Have a bad month? You still get nothing. That's another thing: working for yourself is highly volatile and unpredictable and that's why some people refer to bipolar depression as 'the entrepreneur's disease'.

Here's another difference: when you work for yourself, none of your friends or relatives will respect the fact that you have to work during the week. 'Oh, he/she works from home, so of course they can come and help me move out of my house/meet for lunch on a Wednesday afternoon'. Never mind that you promised your clients their work would be finished at 4pm. Never mind that you'll now have to work until 5am through the night.

And on the flip side of this, your clients won't respect that your home time is your home time. They'll think nothing of e-mailing you at 5am in the morning on a Sunday to tell you the work you handed in three days ago was rubbish.

And you'll have the same problem: you'll always be tempted to finish a little early on a Friday, or to work a little late on a Wednesday. Goodbye body clock! Goodbye healthy sleep! Goodbye good quality work.

Then there's the fact that working from home means working on your own, with no one around, in the same room you're likely to spend your evening in. You never get to leave this space and you never get any outside interaction or input. Talk about cabin fever! **Heeeeere's Johnny!**

Working from home gives you freedom and that freedom can give you the option to become incredibly healthy, happy and effective. At the same time though, freedom also comes with responsibility. Fail to manage that time well and it can all go wrong…

What You Will Learn

Finding the CEO in You

That's the general idea and an outline of the sorts of things we'll be learning in this section. More specifically though, you will learn:

- What lifestyle design is and what it has to do with your health and your business
- How to apply discipline and structure when you have none
- How to avoid cabin fever
- How to manage your workflow and communicate with your clients and customers
- How to fit the right diet and training regime in around your work
- How to sleep better and see this impact on your productivity
- How to incorporate travel and spending time outside into your work
- How to work from home with your family still there
- How to transition to working for yourself
- How to generate passive income

Overall, by the end of this book you should have the tools to create a business model and an environment that allows you to maximize your health, your happiness and your productivity. If you already have a home business, you can use this advice to restructure your routine and setup to support a happier and healthier you.

Are you Happy

If you don't, then you can use this book to give you the confidence and the know-how to take the leap in a way that will have the very best outcome for you.

After all we are creating the CEO of your life but also that of your business.

~Thoughts~

Finding the CEO in You

Chapter 2
Create your Smart Lifestyle Design

I briefly touched on the idea of lifestyle design. What does this mean precisely?

The term 'lifestyle design' was either coined or popularized by Tim Ferriss in his book The Four Hour Workweek. The idea behind it is simple: you create the lifestyle you want out of your job.

This simply means that you think about the lifestyle you want and then you choose a career/build a business to support that.

For most of us, this works in the entirely opposite way. Most of us will find ourselves 'landing in a job' and from there we then see the rest of our lifestyles forming around that. We get a job and right away that dictates where we are going to live, so we normally move to that area.

At the same time, it tells us which hours we are going to work and depending on how far away we live, this will also have to include some time for a commute.

Some people will move away from their friends and family so that they can work the job they have or will even breakup relationships that were otherwise going well – all because of their jobs! And don't get it confused: these aren't jobs that they've always wanted. These aren't 'dream careers' that they have been thinking about since a young age.

No, these are jobs that they 'just kind of landed in' and are now too afraid to leave. And they're completely dictating their lives.

Lifestyle Design: The Alternative

So how does lifestyle design work in principle?

You start out by asking:

"What type of life do I want?"

_____
_____
_____
_____

And from there, you then ask:
"What type of job would best facilitate that lifestyle?

_____
_____
_____
_____

If you want to spend more time with family, if you want to work while travelling the world, if you want to have a career that you find fascinating and that you're proud of… then often the first step to achieving the right lifestyle will be starting to work for yourself and online/from home.

Next you have to ask whether you want to be a busy 'high flier' or whether you'd be happier as someone whose career was 'light', flexible and would largely run itself a lot of the time. This is an important point. Many people make the mistake of thinking they want to be 'really successful' in the most stereotypical of senses and as such they create business plans that involve taking on large numbers of staff with branches all over the world. The reality of being involved in this type of business though is that you now have no time to do things that contribute to a happy and healthy life. Likewise, you now are just as stressed and as tied down – if not moreso – than you would have been if you were working for a big organization in an office.

If you want to be a high profile businessman/woman then that's great. If not, then you need to rethink your business plan. If you want to take it even further in the other direction and live the most relaxed lifestyle possible, then ideally you want some kind of passive income – meaning that you generate money while you sleep. This might mean selling a digital product or it might mean hiring a manager to run the day-to-day elements of your business. Either way, a business that 'runs itself' allows you to live the life you want and to reap the rewards for your hard work later on.

Digital Nomad? Or Digital Homebody

Perhaps one of the ultimate expressions of lifestyle design is to become a digital nomad. In fact, to many people these two terms are synonymous and interchangeable.

A digital nomad essentially is someone who works online so that they are not dependent on a physical location for their career and income. They then are free to go ahead with their lifestyle design but rather than just being content to spend more time at home, they aim bigger and travel the world.

Finding the CEO in You

The archetypal image of the digital nomad is someone sitting by a huge waterfall in the middle of nowhere, typing on their laptop. Or perhaps it's of someone sitting on the beach, sipping cocktails and firing off e-mails to their clients.

This is of course highly appealing for many of us and is certainly a way of living that is more 'free' than what most of us are used to. This way, you can see the world, meet new people and take each day as it comes – never knowing where you're going to end up.

That's an exciting prospect and certainly it can lead to a healthy attitude to life (and tan for that matter) for many of us. However, it also certainly is not for everyone.

Why? Because for starters, you'll be travelling with just a backpack and you'll never get the chance to have a proper bath and to change into fresh clothes that you washed with fabric softener. Likewise, if you're partial to a cup of tea/coffee with milk… good luck getting it.

Also, you can't have a pet dog. And for that matter, a relationship really. You'll be away from your friends and family and it will be scary. Travelling permanently can be very stressful in itself and you'll spend a lot of time in dodgy hostels worrying about your laptop.

But you don't have to take an 'all or nothing' approach to being a digital nomad. Instead, you can travel the world in short bursts. Or you can go on lengthy 'staycations'. Or you can just do three holidays a year instead of one.

Travelling isn't that expensive anymore. If you fly short haul then you can go to some pretty exotic places for $50 and if you are smart about when and how you buy, you can also travel a long way on the train relatively cheaply. While you're travelling, you can be working on your computer and that means you can earn some (or all) of your money back. Remember too: you can travel during the quieter times when everyone else is at work, meaning quieter resorts and lower prices.

Then, you can be working in a chalet in France, or at your friend's house in Mexico. And you can do this for four or five days, several times a year and still feel like you're getting to experience more of life than your office-bound friends. At the same time though, when you start to miss home, you can travel back and cuddle up with your wife and kids by the fire.

With smart lifestyle design, you can have your cake and eat it!

What is a Digital Nomad?

So just what is a digital nomad?

Essentially, becoming a digital nomad is your way out. This is how you escape the rat race and start to see the world. A digital nomad is someone who works online and who uses that style of work in order to be able to travel, see the world and live a life of adventure.

Sounds too good to be true right?

But it makes perfect sense. Today, travel is cheaper than it has ever been. Budget airlines make it incredibly affordable to visit countries all over the world, while trains and coaches connect land within continents.

Then you have things like AirBnB and Couchsurfing – sites that make it even cheaper to find accommodation abroad and to really live as a part of the country you're in.

Meanwhile, more and more people are starting to earn a living online. Many businesses are allowing their employees to work remotely, using tools like video conferencing software and collaboration software in order to stay in touch and continue working as part of the team.

Those with an entrepreneurial streak meanwhile can just as easily make money from selling services online as web developers, writers, photographers or coders. Or they can create their own businesses that can be run from anywhere in the world: blogs for example, or affiliate marketing schemes.

And when you marry these two developments, it means that there is no longer any need to work from a small crowded office. You can take your work with you on the road and that road is open to more people than ever before.

Nothing is keeping you trapped in your current lifestyle. Nothing is stopping you from throwing on a backpack and heading out that door, to begin a lifetime of adventure and travel.

Of course there are going to be a few challenges and struggles along the way. How do you travel if you have a family for example? How do you transition to working online? And how do you ensure that you're able to stay productive when you're lost in another country?

We'll be answering all those questions in this book, so sit back, grab a cup of coffee and let's spend the next hour or so learning how you can become truly free again.

Just as you were always meant to be.

The Top Benefits of Being a Digital Nomad

You'll be able to travel the world

You'll have incredible experiences

You'll meet amazing and diverse people

Are you Happy

- You'll have legendary stories to tell

- You'll grow as a person

- You'll develop your skills as an entrepreneur

- You'll have a taste of true freedom

- You'll be able to do work that you find truly enjoyable and rewarding

- You'll learn to become completely self-reliant

- You'll learn more about yourself and about what you really need to be happy

- You'll be joining a huge, growing community of like-minded individuals

- You'll be a pioneer – working in a fashion that would have been unthinkable even a decade ago

- You'll improve your happiness, your health and your perspective

Unchain Yourself

When you become a digital nomad, you'll find there are good times and bad times. It's important to have a balanced idea of what this is really going to entail and what life as a nomad is really like. We'll talk about the struggles and tribulations of the digital nomad lifestyle later on. Suffice to say, that this is not a lifestyle that will be for everyone. And that's okay.

But for many, the positives are going to greatly outweigh the negatives. The feeling of true freedom, of being able to go anywhere you wish in an incredible foreign land… that's something that can't be understated.

Finding the CEO in You

There will be moments as a digital nomad where everything just clicks into place. Really magical moments that stay with you forever.

Sometimes, these moments will be moments with other people. Imagine sitting in a hanging chair with a beautiful girl/guy and listening to the sea lapping against the shore. You realize you have a lot in common and the night ends with you kissing under the stars, as you hear the distant sounds of a bar not far away.

Other times, these moments will be those moments of adventure and exploration. Imagine coming up over the top of a hill to realize that you've just discovered and incredible view from the top of a mountain – an absolutely breathtaking view.

How often does your 9-5 lifestyle allow for moments like this?

But other times, the moments are going to be much smaller. Sometimes you'll get these moments while you're working in a bar. People are passing by on the wet, cobbled streets outside and you're busily working away, listening to bar music and sipping a local beer while you work. The lights are neon and you're feeling inspired.

What incredible moments.

This is what you're working for as a digital nomad. This is why you're going to go through the challenges. This is why you must overcome the obstacles standing in your way.

The Cognitive Shift: Lifestyle Design

The first step to becoming a digital nomad is to make the cognitive shift in your own mind – to start viewing yourself differently and to start changing the way you consider your priorities

Are you Happy

and your commitments. We have been taught that certain variables in our lives are unchangeable. That there is just one way of doing things.

Of course this is not the case though. And actually, if you're willing to be creative, you can play with these elements anyway you choose. Before you make this realization, internalize it and make it a part of your philosophy, you're going to struggle to truly make the necessary changes to becoming a digital nomad.

The first thing you need to realize for instance, is that you need to start 'working to live' rather than 'living to work'. Likewise, recognize that work in and of itself is not what should give your life value.

Imagine that you could earn the same salary doing a job like rubbish collection. The job isn't particularly rewarding, there isn't a lot of career progression… but you can be finished by 4pm and you never bring your work home with you.

Do you take the job?

A lot of people will answer 'no'. Why? Because they feel they wouldn't get a sense of reward from that work. They wouldn't feel successful, or like they were progressing.

But the question to ask yourself, is why you are getting your sense of reward and progression from your job to begin with.

Why is this the only way you can feel like you're doing something worthwhile?

This is one of the factors that makes people take on more and more responsibility and work harder and harder, just to feel like they're 'successful'.

But instead, why not be successful by writing a book? Why not be successful by making art? Or by travelling the world?

Why not get your sense of purpose and reward from the things you do outside your office?

People tend to feel very proud about working hard but what value does working hard truly have? When the only result of that hard work is that a stapler gets delivered on time? Is that really what you want to measure success in your life by?

Instead then, ask yourself what it is that you really want from life. What do you want to achieve? What would make you truly happy?

Then just think about what the easiest way to get to that point is.

This way of thinking is known as 'lifestyle design' and it's the quickest way to improve your happiness and to get the very most out of life.

An Introduction to Lifestyle Design

To begin using lifestyle design in your own life, the first thing you need to do is to decide what it is that you want to try and achieve in your life. What is your passion? What gives you a sense of drive and motivation?

To discover the answer, try picturing and visualizing the ideal life for yourself. What does it entail?

Maybe your perfect life involves living in a massive house, having your own pool and spending lots of time relaxing?

Or maybe your perfect life involves spending more time with your friends and family? Maybe it involves creating music? Or maybe it involves travelling and seeing the world?

Where do you picture yourself living?

Are you Happy

Who do you picture yourself living with?

What are you spending your income on?

The next thing to do, is to start thinking about what the easiest and most effective way to accomplish those things is. And what is the best job when it comes to supporting that lifestyle?

THIS is what a job should be. It should be the thing that best enables you to live the lifestyle that makes you happiest. It should support your life, not dictate it.

And yet so many people will come home late because their work demands it, or move to other parts of the country!

Once you realize that your job should support your lifestyle, you might realize that actually, you'd be much happier if you didn't have an hour long commute.

Actually, you'd be much happier if you weren't stressed after work.

And actually, you only need X amount of money in order to support your lifestyle.

Meanwhile, you can reduce your outgoings in order to become 'wealthier' on a lower salary (and to have more money to spend on the things that matter to you) and you can make other changes in your life – like moving to another part of the world.

Follow your passion and don't let your job derail you.

Becoming a digital nomad is just one example of lifestyle design. In this case, the lifestyle you are designing simply revolves around travel and adventure. And by choosing the right career, you're able to support that lifestyle and make it possible.

You CAN have your cake and eat it.

You DON'T have to play by the rules.

And you DON'T have to live a 'conventional' lifestyle.

Preparing for Your Journey

This is the realization you need to come to before you can start making progress toward a digital nomad lifestyle. This is what is going to empower you to make the necessary changes that will set you on that path.

For example, you may find that the best way to embrace the digital nomad lifestyle is to quit your day job.

This is something that many of us will struggle with.

A LOT.

But the reality is that there's no reason you can't do it or shouldn't do it. The worst case scenario is that your online work doesn't work out and in that case, you just need to find work again.

That's the worst case scenario.

The alternative is to carry on working where you are, to never try and make the change and to continue being unhappy. Suddenly, that risk doesn't seem like such a big one!

Many people will feel like they are throwing away their careers but if it's not a career you're passionate about… then who cares?

Your family will support you if things don't work out and at least you will have tried. It's better to fail at trying something exciting than to succeed at doing nothing at all…

Are you Happy

To find a career that will support your digital nomad existence, you first need to calculate how much you are likely to spend, which tells you how much you need to earn. You can then look at ways of bringing down that expense (it's not all about how much you earn). Are you willing to couch surf? Are there some cheaper places you can visit to start with?

Are you able to lease your own property to bring in a side salary/pay for your mortgage?

Are you willing to eat into some of your savings, if it means that you're going to have the most incredible experience that you'll remember for the rest of your life?

What will you do when you want to come home? Do you ever want to come home?

When considering all this, it's going to be scary. It's not what we've been brought up to do. It's not how we're taught to think.

It's probably not a good time…

Know this though: it is never a good time! You either do it now, or you don't do it.
And no matter what your circumstances, there are ways to get around it when you make your quality of life your priority.

Come up with a plan for what you want to do and how you want to live and then you'll be able to start creating the income you need to support those lifestyle decisions.

Once you have your plan and you have the resolve to commit to it, the next thing to think about is how you're going to make it work.

And more specifically, how you're going to fund your travels and your lifestyle.

There are plenty of options and we're going to look at a few of those in the coming chapters…

Go Online for Remote Jobs

One thing you can do, is to continue working your current job. The difference of course is that you're going to have to go 'remote'.

This is again something that a lot of us will feel anxious about. We won't want to ask our bosses if it's possible for fear of upsetting the apple cart.

But at the end of the day, it's always worth asking and it certainly can't hurt. With video conferencing and collaboration tools, it's now easier than ever to manage the majority of jobs abroad and you can even find online 'time clock' software to help you clock in and out, among other things.

Speak with your current manager or boss about the possibility of working from home to begin with, trial it if they say yes, and then try to take that to the next logical point and see if you can get them to let you work abroad – it will be no different.

Some companies are of course going to dismiss this idea out of hand. There are legitimate reasons why some jobs can't be carried out in another country. For instance, if you're in a customer-facing job, then you might find that you're not able to work online. Likewise, you may well find that you can't very easily work online if your job involves operating a switch board and answering lots of calls. Perhaps you need to be logged into the network. Maybe you need to be at work during particular hours – World Time Buddy can help you to sync your clock with home but it won't help if their 3pm is your 3am!

But don't give up right away. If they say no at first, then you can often find a workaround by compromising. Ask if there are any other jobs you can do within the organization that would allow you to travel. If they still say no, then ask if you could do part-time work, or even freelance for them.

Are you Happy

Simply express your desire to work remotely, explain that you want to travel and see the world and then discuss to see if you can find an arrangement that works for all parties involved. At the end of the day, they will likely want to help you work in a way that you find rewarding and will probably be more flexible than you'd expect.

If they want to keep you, then they'd rather you worked flexibly than left completely!

Note: Be ready to demonstrate how you can do your work just as well remotely. The onus is on you to make this work, so make sure they can see that you're able to work online while still doing the same amount you normally would. That means researching the software solutions and more, if necessary.

Find Another Job

Can't work from home at your current job?

Not sure you want the responsibility and potential risk of running your own business?

Another straightforward solution is simply to find another job that will allow you to work how you want! Obviously there are some industries that are more likely to let you do this than others, so that's a good starting point. You could work for a web design company for example and in all likelihood, they'll let you work online. Likewise, you could become a journalist for a magazine – there little reason you can't do that work remotely. Many big companies like WordPress are distributed around the entire world and more than happy to let you work from wherever you choose.

Often, job descriptions will mention that you can work from home.

And if they don't, then you can call or write in to enquire.

This is a good option because it guarantees you'll have a stable income before you give up your current job. Just hunt around for a more flexible one and then leave! Remember: this might mean taking a pay cut or moving down the hierarchy. But that's okay!

Find Your Own Work

Another way to go about this, is to approach businesses you'd like to work for and that operate predominantly online. For example, if you are a regular reader of a big blog, then you can always try contacting the editor and asking them if you can work for them.

As I alluded to earlier, you can also work online as a sports commentator! A friend of mine does this job and it essentially involves getting paid to watch his team play and write about it in real-time. This is something he found simply by looking at the website of a sports site he went to regularly and spotting that they were advertising for work.

These days, more and more companies operate online like this and advertise for full or part-time employees. Take a look around and even try googling 'Work for Us' and other terms that might bring up a result!

Start Your Own Online Business or Micro Business

While all the above is true, the predominant way that most people will earn while they travel is by working online with their own business. This gives you more freedom over how, where and when you work which in turn means you can spend more time doing incredible things or working in incredible spots!

Earning Money as a Freelancer

Are you Happy

The most obvious way to run a business online is to freelance. Freelance work simply means going out and looking for clients and then completing work for them at a time that suits you.

Normally when you do this, you'll be working to a deadline. Around that deadline though, it will be up to you how you want to work and this is what will give you the freedom to travel as you wish and work when you wish.

There are plenty of services you can provide online as a freelancer and these include:

- Writing
- Editing
- Web design
- Coding
- Video production
- Consultation
- Personal training (over Skype for instance)
- Marketing
- Promotion
- Career guidance
- Virtual assistant services
- Data entry
- Admin
- Moderation

- Sports commenting

- And much more!

Once you decide what it is you want to do, all you need to do then is to start finding the work. To give yourself the most stable income and the most flexibility to work and travel, you want to minimize the admin and the comms – so try finding a few big clients and sticking with them (offer bulk discounts and reduced rates for repeat customers).

Start off by looking for people you know you can work with and if you don't have any such contacts, then try looking online at 'freelancing sites' like UpWork. On this site, people advertise for work and advertise for services.

Another option is to look on 'webmaster forums'. These are forums where people discuss internet marketing and website management. If you head onto these sites, then you can advertise your work and often find websites that need skills like graphic design or copywriting.

Or how about visiting '#Nomads'. This is a website and online community that supports digital nomads and provides them with an easy means to find work, discuss the lifestyle and more.

Selling Services

Being a freelancer is one way you can make money selling a service online. Actually though, there are also several others and not every option has to be B2B necessarily.

In fact, many of the services you might traditionally have provided face to face can now be provided online!

How about offering personal training for example? All you need to do is to find clients and then consult with them over Skype. You could even offer extra services like texts to remind them to go to the gym etc.

What about a dating agency? Let people come to you and then help them polish up their dating profile and more? For something like this, all you need is a consultation session and then perhaps access to their dating profiles.

You could be a lifestyle coach too. Or a business consultant. In fact, you can even offer a lot of services as a lawyer online! This could mean offering affordable legal advice or even handling things like conveyancing. I bought a house recently and I never once had to meet my conveyancing lawyer… And this is especially easy thanks to many of the modern tools, apps and services available once again. Docusign for example makes it easy to sign documents over the web!

In many cases you might find that you can do your current job in this fashion. If you currently work for a Virgin Active gym, then just tell your favourite clients that you're going freelance and that they can cheaply access your services online!

Cut hair? How about telling your current clients that you'll be running a style consultation service online that they can access via Skype if they want to?

Be creative, think outside the box and really you can do any job that doesn't require you to be physically present!

Creating Passive Income

While finding clients and providing a service online is a great way to experience the freedom to work from anywhere and whenever you like, it is still ultimately very restricting in other ways. At the end of the day, you still need to meet your deadlines and to all extents and purposes, you still have 'bosses' who will be unhappy if you don't completely your work to a good standard.

Finding the CEO in You

When you work a service, you're going to have to balance your time between travelling and exploring these different countries while at the same time also trying to get enough work done. When you can't find a plug socket, or when you have too much you want to see and do… this can be a big cause of stress.

And it's for that reason that you might consider creating a passive income business model instead. This is essentially a business model that will generate income without you having to actively work on it.

That is not to say that you're making money for doing nothing. Rather, it means you're putting in some work up front and then profiting for a while to come afterward.

How can this possibly work? There are a few strategies you can use…

Sell a digital product – Digital products are products like ebooks and digital courses that don't require any work on your part to produce. You create them once and from there, you can then sell them as many times as you want. There's no delivery to worry about and no storage! There are plenty of examples of how this can work, but you can sell from your own web page and send traffic there with an advertising campaign, you can sell something like an app or a Kindle ebook through a ready-made distribution network (the Kindle Store or the iTunes Store), or you can let other marketers promote your product for commission.

Affiliate marketing – This means that you're selling a product you didn't make and getting commission. Many creators are happy to offer as much as 75% of their profits to try and encourage more people to help them sell and this means you can make almost as much money as you would do from your own product – but with no need to create anything! You just make a landing page and then advertise it to get people to buy through your referral link.

Are you Happy

Service arbitrage – Service arbitrage essentially means that you are buying and selling a service and profiting simply by taking advantage of differences in market prices. For example, many Indian web designers are happy to charge a small amount in US dollars because the money will go further in their home country. That makes them highly competitive with US web design companies. What you can do then, is to find web design clients and then hire the Indian web company to complete the work on your behalf. You simply take a little off the top and pocket the difference! The best thing about this method of making money is that a lot of smaller companies actually expect you to resell their work and are happy to have you simply passing on the orders. These are called 'white label services' and they essentially act like ghost writers! Ghost web designers…

Dropshipping – Dropshipping is a way that you can sell physical products, perhaps through an online ecommerce store – and not actually have to deliver them! You do this by finding wholesalers that offer fulfilment services. They will split the profits with you and handle everything from the storage to the delivery. Best of all, is that they once again are often happy to be 'white label' meaning that the people you deal with won't even know they exist. That means that they will feel as though they're buying directly from you!

Creating Content

Somewhere in-between passive income and providing a service is to run a blog, a website or a YouTube channel. Doing this allows you to build your own audience of loyal followers and then profit from advertising, sponsorship or even sales of a digital product.

This isn't truly passive income because you'll still need to regularly update the site. But you are not beholden to any deadlines other than the ones you set and this means that you can work at a pace that is comfortable for you. Want to take the day of to explore the Roman Forum? No one will stop you.

This is actually the ideal scenario because now you'll be earning money by doing a job that you truly feel passionate about. You'll
have the satisfaction of having online 'followers' and fans and you'll be able to build a name for yourself that could potentially be very profitable.

The downside is that this type of work takes the longest to have any success with. Everyone wants to make money from a blog but not everyone is successful! This takes a lot of patience, a lot of smarts and a fair bit of luck. But it's definitely do-able!

The key is to provide real value, to do something different from everyone else and to spend enough time and effort necessary to swamp the search engines and social media with content.

The great news though? You now have a perfect topic to blog about. Travel and the digital nomad lifestyle are hot topics right now and you'll have the 'value proposition' and desirable lifestyle to really help build an enthusiastic following and encourage some sales. This is such a great and easy lifestyle to promote: post a picture of yourself working on the beach with an incredible sunset in the background and that's the kind of thing that gets followers!

Note: There are many other ways that you can use your lifestyle to help you find more work too. For example, you can sell photographs of the scenery or the wildlife where you are and you'll find it's very easy to find buyers! Or how about travel writing for a magazine or publishing company?

Getting All Your Ducks in a Row

You know what kind of travel you want to do, you have your online work set up and you have the tools and skills you need to work on the road.

Are you Happy

Are you ready to go yet? Not quite I'm afraid! You still need to sort out the legality of your travel, the finances and your travel kit! But don't worry, I'm going to walk you through it…

The reality is that you're going to find you have no problem a lot of the time… and that you really struggle every now and then! On my own travels, I have worked outdoors on my phone with my folding keyboard in the rain and I've begged receptionists in hotels to send files from my SD cards. These things happen but actually, that's part of the fun of being a digital nomad!

And you will be very surprised some of the places you can find free WiFi! You'll struggle in London unless you can find a library or coffee shop (try huddling in the doorway!) but up a mountain in Croatia with not a sign of life nearby? No problem!

(This is not a random example but rather something I actually experienced when working in Krka national park! Beautiful waterfalls there and definitely worth checking out…)

Your Travel Kit Bag

First of all, you'll need to bring a lot more than just items that you can use to get work done. Remember, the point of this trip is to have a good time – not just to work! So you need to bring things that will make the trip as comfortable as possible, as well.

Some important considerations include:

Your Bag

Of course the bag itself is going to be one of the most important things you can bring with you as a digital nomad! Specifically, you are going to want a backpack and this should be one that you can use to store lots of things while staying comfortable. Look for breathable meshes on the back, look for padded straps and look for waist belts. This will all help when you're trekking up a mountain or across a dessert!

Finding the CEO in You

The bag should also have plenty of pockets, including concealed pockets. I personally take two bags, one of which is actually a 'chest bag' that is intended for use by anglers. The benefit of this is that I can keep important documents where I can see them and even fit in a small 8" computer. Yet you'll find that airlines don't count this as an additional item of hand-luggage… win!

Clothes

When packing clothes, it's important think 'small, light and

versatile'. Create a capsule wardrobe so that every item can be worn with every other item without looking awful and choose things that ideally don't need to be ironed. It is possible to get non-iron shirts from companies like Mizzen and Main and these look brilliant even when they've been rolled into a ball…

And rolling your shirts into a ball is a great tip – it takes up much less space that way!

Kindle

A Kindle is an incredibly useful gadget to take with you on holiday that will give you infinite reading material while taking up barely any space.

The best part is that if you get a generation 1 or 2 Kindle, then you'll also get an experimental browser with free 3G coverage all around the world! How is that for a digital nomad secret? Bring this with you and you'll be

Documents and Practical Considerations

When you go on holiday, there are a few things you need to consider: visas, documents and travel insurance for example.

So it only stands to follow that when you go travelling for an indefinite time period, there is far more to sort out. And doing this

Are you Happy

before you leave – getting all your ducks in a row - is going to help you to reduce stress and avoid problems while you're on the road!

Follow this check-list to get everything straight:

Travel Insurance

If you're travelling abroad, then you should always take out travel insurance. You'll want something fairly comprehensive that will allow you to hop continents, engage in sports and other activities and cover the cost of your belongings.

The good news is that it's easy these days to get travel insurance online and on your mobile – and many of these apps will let you update your policy as you travel to adapt to your changing requirements!

Bills and Post

If you're going to be away from your home for 3 months or more, then you need to make sure that your post isn't going to pile up. Not only will this make it apparent that you're away but it will also mean that you might miss an important bill. Make sure that you set up forwarding on your address and have your mail sent to a good friend or your parents. Let them open those letters and they can update you on anything important.

Meanwhile, you can ask many service providers and banks to send their statements and bills digitally. This saves paper and makes life easier for you.

Of course you should also cancel magazine subscriptions, broadband, cable TV and anything else that you're not going to need!

Legalities

If you're spending more than a few months in any country, then you might need a visa. In fact, you're likely to need a visa even to enter some countries.

And what's more, is that you need to check with your own local law as to whether there's a maximum time you can remain out of the country (in which case you might need to make temporary return visits). You'll need to find out if you need to pay council tax in different countries, whether you're allowed to get jobs abroad and more.

All of this is important to research before you set sail. There are few things more stressful than being on a plane only to hear an announcement that you need a visa to enter the country that you don't have!

Phone

As mentioned already, it's important to ensure that you'll have phone coverage abroad. Speak with your mobile provider and ask what their best options are for people who travel a lot. Data roaming and having a lot of data is particularly important so you can tether to your mobile when you need to.

You may also want to forward calls to your home to your mobile! House Care

If you're leaving a house empty, then consider discussing with a friend or family member if they would be willing to come in and look after your plants occasionally, or perhaps turn the lights on to make it look like someone is home!

Another tip is to consider setting up a remote digital camera in your home so that you can check on it from abroad. This is a great way to get peace of mind when you're worrying!

Your Travel Documents Pack

If you're going abroad then there will almost always be a plethora of different documents you need to bring with you. That will not only mean your passport (which you need to ensure is up-to-date) but it will also mean your boarding pass, your hotel confirmation, any maps that you need etc.

Print all this information out, make multiple copies and then stick them in your various bags to bring with you. Print more information than you need and make sure you have hard copies as well as digital in case your phone fails you.

Preparing Your Finances

You've got your documents and your bag ready, your online business is set-up and ready to go and you have a good knowledge of where you're going.

Now you just need to worry about your money… Cash and Cheques – What to Bring?

There's no way that you can bring all the cash you're going to need for an indefinitely long journey with you! For that reason then, you'll need to bring cards, cheques and more.

At any given point, you should have enough money to last you about a week. This will ensure that you won't get into trouble if you should lose your card and you'll still be able to get home or at least stay a few nights in a hostel.

Another tip is to keep a little cash separate and safe. For example, try keeping some in your shoe and that way, even if your things get stolen, you'll have some cash to get by! You can also try using travellers' cheques. These can be cashed in abroad but require ID, which means they're useless to anyone who steels them from you.

Finding the CEO in You

If you have life savings, then make sure it is very difficult for anyone who gets hold of your things to access them. Security is a big issue when you travel.

Bank

You'll need to let your bank know that you're no longer at your current address and you'll probably want to use a parent or friend's address instead.

You also need to speak with your bank about withdrawing cash. Make sure you're with a bank that makes it easy for you to get money out abroad and consider switching if yours carries a hefty fee.

Better yet is to get a credit card. Not only do these work abroad but they also protect you against having your cash stolen. Because the money isn't yours, it will be on the credit card company to chase it up!

Another tip is to consider getting a PayPal card. This again gives you an extra layer of security by allowing you to shop without handing over bank details. And better yet, you're likely to get paid by many clients online through PayPal. Thus the money never needs to even visit your bank account!

Financing

The hope of course is that you're going to earn money online in order to finance your trip but it can also be useful to have other income streams. One, as mentioned, is to rent out your home, in which case you'll probably want to use a property management company to handle the day-to-day administration and you'll need a storage unit to keep your things. You'll likewise need to find storage if you are renting and you're not going to have anywhere to come back to!

Another option is to take out a loan. This might seem reckless but again, the way to look at it is as spending money on what is likely to be one of the most amazing and transformative experiences of your life. It's far from reckless or a waste.

And a good option here is to get a PayPal loan! This works very well with the PayPal card option (because you'll be able to fill your PayPal account without worrying about withdrawing), it has zero impact on your credit rating and you will be able to pay it back out of payments you receive from clients and customers! In other words, you'll only need to pay it back as your online earnings are working out.

You don't need to have a big lump sum of money to go travelling like this but if you can get some from PayPal or another source, then it will free you to explore more openly and worry less about cash!

Budgeting

Finally, it is always a good idea to plan your trip and to pay careful attention to your budgeting as you do. Plot a route through countries you wish to visit while ensuring that you're going to be able to afford to visit them on the salary you're likely to be earning!

Again, try looking for ways to cut cost – such as using SkyScanner to find the cheapest flights, AirBnB and Couchsurfing. There is a resource sheet that comes with this ebook and if you check that, you'll find plenty of excellent tools to help you plot your trip and save money on the road!

Are You Ready for the Journey of a Lifetime?

But if you do decide that this lifestyle is for you, then you're going to need to finalize your plans and get ready to set off!

All that's left to do is to finalize your travel arrangements…

Plot a course between different countries – start by thinking about the type of travel you want to do, then list the things you'd like to see.

Finding the CEO in You

Consider using travel groups, meditation retreats, conservation resorts and more. This will give you the opportunity to meet more people and to find things you wouldn't otherwise

Look at forums and find insider tips on where to visit Book your travel using the tools we've recommended (SkyScanner, AirBnB, Couchsurfing) and other sites like Expedia and Hotels.com.

Research visas and anything else you're going to need Print everything out

Make sure to leave leeway – book the start of your journey but for later portions, just research some options rather than having anything set in stone. Discuss accommodation with Couchsurfing users but tell them you may yet cancel.

Download all the apps and tools you're likely to use, buy the hardware you're going to need

Try to mix your hotels and hostels. Sleeping rough several nights will help you to save cash, while spending a few nights in nice hotels will let you recharge your batteries (literally as well!)

Tell people you're going, pay off debts, cancel your bills…

Count down the days!

Hopefully you're now brimming with excitement and your mind is racing with possibilities. Where will you go? What will you see? The possibilities are truly endless and you really don't need to be a nomad in the 'typical sense'. Remember: lifestyle design is about living the life you want to lead and not travelling to developing countries or the middle of Africa because you think that's what you are 'meant to be doing'. If your idea of being a nomad is to live in nice log cabins, driving from destination to destination… then go for it!

Are you Happy

And as we mentioned, you don't even need to leave the country necessarily to be a 'nomad'. The world is your oyster. You are truly free!

The hardest part though is always going to be taking that first step and making the leap – making the decision to start putting your life first. And being bold enough to quit a good job.

But here's one last invaluable tip: it doesn't have to be binary. You don't need to become a nomad overnight. Why not set up an online business using some annual leave over the course of a week? See how much money you can earn? You can then run it in the evenings and on the weekends, maybe even trial travelling as you do it.

And then only if it works do you need to quit your job and actually set off!

The sky is the limit but you have to take the leap.

~Thoughts~

_____
_____
_____
_____
_____
_____
_____
_____
_____
_____
_____
_____
_____
_____

Finding the CEO in You

Chapter 23
Set-Up your Work Culture

This following chapter is going to be aimed mainly at those who choose not to go the digital nomad route. Either you're someone who is content to just have more freedom working from home, or you're working from home part of the time and travelling when the opportunity presents itself.

Either way, the rest of the time you're going to need somewhere to work and you're going to need some structure. If you're already working from home, then you should read the following chapter carefully and perhaps modify some of your current routine/setup. If you're planning on working from home, then you should use this when creating your business model and the parameters for your productivity.

Your Work Environment

Before you can start working from home, the first thing you need to ask yourself is where you will actually be working. In other words, where will you be physically located as you type/answer e-mails/program.

Remember: we're focused on creating a lifestyle and a business model that will support health, happiness and productivity. Where you're working is a big part of this and being able to decide on the specifics of your work environment is one of the big advantages of working for yourself. So make the most of it!

Working From Home, But Not From Home

The first point to bear in mind here is that working from home doesn't have to mean working from home. We've already seen that when we discussed becoming a 'digital nomad'. You can take a similar approach more locally though too, by just taking a laptop out with you and working in local coffee shops or libraries.

This has a lot of advantages as compared with working from an office in your own home. For starters, when you work in a coffee shop, you get to leave the house. This is important because it psychologically separates your work life from your home life and makes it that little bit easier for you to 'switch off' when you get home. At the same time, it also means you will be taking some steps. Remember: it is recommended that we take at least 10,000 steps a day and failing to do so is bad for your heart leading to a shorter life and causes obesity and back problems.

Another benefit is that this way you also get to meet people. Again, this is quite an important point because spending all your time at home on your own can leave you feeling a little restless and isn't terribly healthy. By heading out to a coffee shop on the other hand, you will get to at least be around other people who are working and you'll get to interact with the baristas who work there.

If you want to go one step further, you can also look into a shared workspace. There are lots of these kinds of initiatives around these days and especially in larger towns. Not only do these then offer you the chance to get out of the house, but you'll also get to spend time with people who are there doing something similar to you. This creates networking opportunities and furthermore means the working environment will be entirely geared towards the kind of work you are doing. That means you'll get good wi-fi and peace and quiet as standard. Some shared work-spaces even give you your own landline and PO Box.

There are other options for where you want to work too – for instance you could always head to a quiet pub or even a bar, or you could sit outside when the weather is nice. Sitting outside is of course great from a health perspective but unfortunately is somewhat lacking in terms of practicality and convenience. To do this well, you'll need to contend with glare on the screen, the lack of somewhere to sit and prop your laptop, bugs, dirt, grass and no power or wifi. Still though, perhaps there's somewhere near you that accounts for all this? Maybe you have a bar with some outside seating that's quiet during the day and faces the beach? The world is your oyster when you work 'from home'.

Setting Up a 'Mobile Command Center'

If you're going to work wherever you like though (or become a digital nomad), then you're going to need to have something to work with. Any small laptop will do the trick and should slip snugly into a shoulder bag or a backpack. You may be limited in terms of the operating system you can use but if not, the MacBook Airs are particularly light and convenient as are Chromebooks (the latter are also very affordable).

For Windows users, the Surface Pro 3 is a fantastic portable machine. This device is essentially a tablet with a slim keyboard built into its cover. It works on your lap (unlike some previous models) and weighs barely anything. What's more, it has beefy specs (up to i7 with 8GB), neat features (particularly the digitizer pen) and a long battery life. The 'Surface 3' (minus the 'Pro') is also very good, being a little smaller and cheaper but
on an Atom processor.

If you want to be even less weighed down, you can go a step further and look at one of the many 8" Windows tablets. With one of these plus a portable Bluetooth keyboard and mouse, you can do pretty much anything you would do on a small ultrabook and never feel weighted down. They tend to have 1-2GB RAM, very long batteries and retail for about $1-200. That means you can take them on a holiday and not worry too much about anything happening to them.

In fact, you can even combine a Surface Pro 3 with an 8" tablet and use it to extend your screen – now you have a multi-monitor setup even in coffee shops! It looks pretty insane and it's great for true productivity on the move.

Creating Your Home Office

On the other hand, you might decide that you do want to work from home. This is fine but you need to be strict about the way you're going to do it to ensure you maintain that separation between your home life and your work life and to keep yourself healthy.

The first tip then is to make sure that your home office really is a home office and not just a table in your living room. Oh and never work in your bedroom. In fact, the ideal scenario is that you only use your bedroom for sleeping and for sex. That way, when you

Are you Happy

head into the room your body and mind will automatically start gearing down for sleep. If you spend part of your day working in the room, then you'll find it's hard to switch off, even when you're under the covers.

For these same reasons, you want to try and choose a room to be your home office that is closed off and that is away from the rest of your property. This way, you can create that separation and it will also mean you're less likely to get disturbed when working from home while your family is there or other people are in the building. Soundproofing is obviously ideal but not necessary.

The next important thing to think about when making your home office is light. Some people actually create 'office pods' these days at the end of their garden, which are mostly-glass sheds that allow them to work as though they're surrounded by nature. You don't have to go that far but do try to let in lots of light and to fill the room with natural things.

Large windows (that are positioned so as not to create glare) and lots of house plants have been shown to help fight depression and stress. What's more, having a 'natural' view can also boost creativity by lowering our heartrate and allowing our minds to wander.

Another important way to maintain your health is to think about the way you'll be sitting. This means making sure that you are upright, with the small of your back well supported by a chair. You should position your monitor so that it is roughly the same height as your eyes with your chin parallel to the floor. If you are looking down all day, you'll develop rounded shoulders and kyphosis. Your hands should be hovering above your keyboard (don't let your wrists rest on the table) and you should be high enough that your elbows are comfortably at a right angle as you type.

If you want to optimize your office for maximum health benefits, then you should also consider getting a standing desk. The best standing desk designs use a collapsing frame that allows you to work either sitting down or standing up. It can be hard to concentrate for long periods while standing, so you might not be able to do this the whole time. However, when you are just answering e-mails or perhaps doing something with design software, standing up can give your back a real break and will help you to burn more calories at the same time.

As for the rest of your home office design, go mad and decorate it however you like. The more color, the more life and the more points of interest, the better. While you might think that sounds distracting, it actually makes your environment much 'richer' from a psychological perspective and that has been linked to triggering 'flow states' – states of intense concentration and high productivity. The more engaging your environment is, the more dopamine and adrenaline you will produce and the more focused you'll be at all times.

Some Health Tips for Working at a Computer

Regardless of whether you're working on a beach in Thailand, from a home office, or at your local coffee shop, there are a couple of health considerations you need to bear in mind which can make a big difference.

Move Regularly

Sitting correctly at the desk, or getting a standing desk can both help you to avoid some of the pitfalls of sitting at a desk all day.

Better yet though? Just move around a lot and that way you'll avoid seizing up and you'll be trying out different positions. If you have a home office, then you should invest in a comfortable chair and desk; but likewise you should also give yourself some alternative places to work whether that's a sofa or it's a beanbag in the corner of the room. Now you'll have the option of switching your position in the room whenever you become uncomfortable.

Also important is just to get up every hour or so, even if just for ten minutes. All this can help to prevent the shortening of your quads, the weakening of your hamstrings and the shortening of your pecs that lead to poor posture, back and knee pain and poor mobility. Moreover, it will help prevent the atrophy of your heart which can significantly shorten your expected lifespan.

Get a Mechanical Keyboard

If you're typing a lot on a daily basis then you open yourself up to repetitive strain injury, arthritis and other issues. A mechanical keyboard can help you to avoid these problems, by giving you something to type on that's specifically designed to be ergonomic, comfortable and supportive. A good mouse can also make a big difference.

Consider Dvorak

Dvorak is an alternative keyboard layout to Qwerty that is said to be more efficient. It essentially puts all of the most commonly used letters in the easiest to reach positions and this in turn can speed up typing while at the same time reducing the risk of arthritis.

It takes a while to learn and the research surrounding Dvorak is not concrete. Nevertheless, if the idea appeals to you then give it a go and you may find it beneficial.

Avoid the Screen at Night

If you're going to be working late into the night – which you may well do despite your best intentions – then you should consider using software to redden the screen, or maybe try wearing 'blue blocking' glasses. Unfortunately, the nature of the wavelength of light produced by most computer monitors is such that the brain mistakes it for sunlight and reacts by producing more cortisol and less melatonin. This makes it much harder for you to sleep and leaves you restful throughout the night; so use these two techniques to avoid that problem.

Protecting Your Eyes

Do you sometimes find yourself wishing you didn't have to look at a screen all the time? Does it give you a headache/make you worry about your eyesight?

Here's the good news: looking at a screen actually isn't bad for your eyes. Studies found that people who sat closer to the computer/TV had worse eyesight but they had the correlation the wrong way round – people sat closer to the screen because of their preexisting poor eyesight. In fact, playing computer games actually improves your visual acuity by forcing you to be aware of your surroundings.

The only danger that comes from looking at computer screens then is caused by glare and changes in brightness. It's going from a very bright screen to a dark object in the room, or going from text with glare to text without glare, that forces the eyes to work hard and readjust focus. This can wear out the muscles and that's when you get headaches.

So make sure that you do work to avoid glare. If you're going to be working on the go make sure your computer has a flexible hinge to avoid direct light and choose your spot carefully. If you're working from home, just make sure you have no windows or lamps in front of the screen. Keep the room you're working in light and if it does get darker, turn the brightness of your monitor down too. Do this and you should find you have no reason anymore to worry about your eyes while working.

~Thoughts~

Are you Happy

Chapter 24
Staying Discipline

If you follow all the advice in the last chapter you should now have a working environment that is conducive to good health and you should know how to avoid some of the common dangers of working from home/at the computer.

What you still need to do as well though, is think about the psychological aspect of your work and the way you're mentally separating one from the other.

This is where so many people who work from home go wrong. We start out with the best of intentions (set working hours, a separate work phone) but the temptation to work late one night, or to work on a Sunday, will always rear its head once we start getting behind. Problem is, this is habit forming and it creates a bad pattern This is especially true if you work late on a weekday, as you'll then have less energy to work again on the next

weekday and that in turn will mean you're tired and lethargic and unproductive… meaning there's a good chance you'll be tempted to work late again. As we'll see later, sleep should be considered sacred if you work from home. And for everyone for that matter…

What you need to do then is to set yourself strict specific parameters for working and to not work outside of those. This means that you have to start working at a very specific time and end at a very specific time. And if you run over and work looks like it's going to be late? Then you have to just accept that it's late. It's not worth ruining your life to keep a client happy – remember the whole reason we're working this way in the first place is to live the lifestyle we want.

Of course it's better that you do also keep your client happy and this is where time management comes in – as well as generally taking the right approach when managing your clients and knowing how to accept work and projects. You also need to put systems in place that will help you to manage a workflow and to become scalable even as an individual. And guess what? That's what we'll be looking at in the rest of this chapter…

Accepting Work

A big challenge as an entrepreneur or as any kind of sole trader is trying to find work. Dry spells are pretty devastating when you have bills to pay and a family telling you to 'get a real job' and if you run a service-based business, no orders means no money.

But what's also a really big challenge is learning to say 'no'. Learning to turn down clients, or to say 'you can have the work in a

Are you Happy

week, I'm busy right now'. We're afraid to do this because we don't want to be in that situation where we have no work but as a result, we end up taking on much more than we can chew and working insane hours that prevent us from sleeping. Worst of all, the work you hand in probably won't be as good as it could be because you'd have been rushed.

So sometimes, you have to be strict and you have to tell your client it will be a few days before you can get work to them. That's okay – in fact it's pretty much normal. As long as you tell them up-front how long it will take, you don't need to feel bad about being just one human. Do your job well and they should normally be able to wait (unless their work is time-sensitive also). If it's a web design, some SEO, an article... a couple of days likely won't make much difference to their business plan.

The same goes for turning down work that you really aren't confident with or that you really don't want to do. Just tell your client that there are others that will do a better job for less money instead of killing yourself trying to learn a whole new skill set. Be strict about what it is that you do and do that one thing very well. You'll be happier, life will be simpler and the quality of your output will be higher.

And in fact, when you tell your clients how long it's going to take, you should actually be pessimistic about it. This is called 'under promising and over delivering' and it basically means saying that things will take longer/cost more/be worse and then providing a pleasant surprise. This strategy is great from a business perspective because it gives you the opportunity to impress your client, which leads to a memorably positive interaction that will make them more likely to want to use your services again.

What's more though, under promising means that if things go wrong and you can't finish work as quickly as you probably should, you'll still have time to get your work in on time the next day. It's a simple strategy that will massively reduce the amount of stress that you find yourself under. And if you're worried you won't get as many orders this way, you can always give an 'expected completion time' and a 'promised completion time' as separate numbers.

Bear in mind that you absolutely cannot rule out the possibility of getting your work in late. There will always be times when things come up unexpectedly – at the very least it's important to remember that you won't get any paid sick leave as someone who is self-employed. (That said, you also mustn't be afraid to occasionally 'phone in sick' with clients as again it's more efficient in the long term).

Choosing Clients

So sometimes you need to turn down work that you get offered or just say you're handing it in late. Other times however, you should turn down entire clients.

That's because there is very much a thing as a 'good client' versus a 'bad client'. Bad clients are the ones who involve too much 'communication overhead' (meaning they e-mail all the time about petty things, ultimately costing you time and money). They're also the ones who pay late (or not at

all) and who are never satisfied with your work. What you'll find is that some clients fit this description, while others are polite and send the minimum number of e-mails necessary for you to work together. It's the latter kind you want to work with as it will ultimately save you a lot of time and stress down the line. Again, picking and choosing clients

is one of the big advantages when it comes to working for yourself.

Another type of client you probably want to lose, is the type who orders tiny amounts of work. The more clients you have with small orders, the more relationships you need to manage, the more projects you have to order and generally the more stressed you are likely to be. This is called 'Pareto's Law' or the '80/20' rule. The idea here is that usually it's just 20% of your customers who provide about 80% of your yields – and that you should focus on that 20% instead of the other 80.

Revenue Streams

All this said, you do want to try and avoid a situation where you have all of your eggs in one basket. In other words, if you turn down all your clients and end up with just one, then you're going to be in a bit of a sticky situation should that one client suddenly quit.

The ideal situation is to try and spread your workload between 3-4 clients. And in terms of income, you should be able to survive relatively well even if you lose two of those clients. The same goes if you're selling a product from your website, or if you're selling an app… have multiple apps and multiple products.

It's even a good idea to have an entirely separate revenue stream. Let's say you're a web designer with several big clients. As a designer you might go some lengthy patches where you don't have any work coming in and as such, you should make sure that you have a monetized website, an app or something else that is bringing in a little extra cash. You could even leave the house some days and offer your services as a fence painter by driving around the neighborhood.

In other words, you need as many revenue streams as possible, you need backup plans and you need contingencies. With all these in place, you'll be less reliant on steady work and you'll thus be less tempted to take on more work than you can manage during the busy periods.

Another tip is to use your quieter days to put work in ahead of time. For instance, if you're a web designer, you can always try designing some unique fonts or some website templates that you can use later on to save yourself time. This way you'll be able to take on more work later on, without feeling overwhelmed.

Targets

While managing all this work, it can be useful to set yourself targets in terms of how much you want to earn. Don't aim too high but make sure that it's something you can realistically live off. Depending on the nature of your work, something like $150 a day is a good 'base rate'.

Having a target like this is a good idea because it allows you to structure everything else accordingly and to decide how much work you're going to take on and at what point in the week you're going to do it. At the same time, you can be sure that you'll be sticking to at least a minimum amount of income without going broke.

Systems

Even with a good balance of clients and no unreal expectations, you'll still likely find that things can get out of hand and you can find yourself stressed. When your client messages you at 8pm on a Friday night saying that the work you did for them isn't very good… how can you possibly ignore it? Likewise, when it turns out the software update you released to your customers had a major bug in it on Friday night… again, what can you do?

There are a few different systems and tools you can put in place that can help you in any of these situations. If you want to find more of these, then I highly recommend the book 'The Four Hour Workweek' from Tim Ferriss which
goes into this sort of thing in-depth.

Are you Happy

However, the ones supplied below should be just enough to help you significantly reduce your stress working from home so that you can start improving your health and happiness...

Auto-Responders

The first and most straightforward tool/system to use is your e-mail's auto-responder capability. This allows you to send an automated reply to your clients, customers and business partners whenever they message you after 6pm or on a weekend and this can say something like this:

"Thank you for your message. I'm afraid I will be out of the office until tomorrow at 9am and will be unable to respond until then. If you have a real emergency, then you can contact me on my home phone number at: 00 0 000000. But please don't call if it can wait until tomorrow.

My working hours are between 9am-6pm Monday-Friday."

This e-mail is perfect because it tells your clients or customers why you haven't gotten back to them and gives them a means to get in touch if they really are in a dire situation. You should find though that very few people will actually abuse your home number, so you can be safe in the knowledge that you'll be undisturbed. That said, you can also stop imagining worst-case scenarios.

Virtual Assistants

A virtual assistant is someone who can handle all types of work on your behalf as long as they don't need to be physically present. Usually these companies/individuals are based in India or in other countries with lower costs of living, so you'll likely only pay a few dollars for a day's work. Of
course you get what you pay for to an extent, so don't expect amazing quality English unless you are willing to pay top dollar.

Either way though, these companies provide work that can include: booking appointments, responding to e-mails, doing research, handling marketing and SEO, proof reading, data entry and much more. You can use a digital assistant then to outsource the boring-but-time consuming aspects of your job, while you focus instead on doing what it is that you do so well. They can also stand-in for you sometimes at the weekend.

Similarly, it never hurts to know a couple of people who can help you out in a crisis. If you have a friend who works online, you can make a pact with them to bail each other out occasionally if you have too much work. You might even be able to offer some aspects of your work to friends interested in making a little extra money on the side!

Automation

There are all kinds of different tools you can use online these days to automate your work. One of the very best of these is IFTTT which essentially allows you to link different online tools and social media accounts together. For instance, IFTTT - https://ifttt.com/ (which stands for 'If This, Then That') can create a system where your Facebook posts are likewise posted to Twitter – this can save you a lot of time in a social media campaign.

But there's much more besides. You can also use this tool to copy all your Gmail contacts to a Google Drive spreadsheet, or to add Google Calendar appointments to a To Do List. IFTTT and many tools like it can act as force multipliers and save you a lot of time.

A Separate Phone

If you use your mobile for work, then it's highly advisable to have a separate mobile for your personal life. This way, you can take that phone and drop it in a drawer at the end of the day. Now you won't be disturbed by e-mails from your clients, or from customers or visitors to your website, because you won't be aware of them.

Hypothesis Testing

All these tools will do a lot to help you spend less time working and to help you 'switch off' at the end of the day. Ultimately though, you're still going to have to 'trust' in the fact that you can take time off of work or not respond immediately to an e-mail and this is the hard part.

This is also the crucial part though. Until you learn to psychologically let go of work, you're not going to get the recovery you need to be healthy and to perform optimally. Even if you aren't getting e-mails, you'll still find work takes its toll if you're lying away thinking about how to apologize to that angry e-mail.

The best way to accomplish this is with a CBT (cognitive behavioral therapy) technique called 'hypothesis testing'. Here, you think about the thing you're afraid to do and you think about what it is that is making you afraid to do it. You're afraid to ignore e-mails or turn down work because you think your clients will abandon you.

To let go of that fear then, you have to try not responding to e-mails sometimes. Give it a go – respond to the next e-mail you get tomorrow instead of right now and then just apologize for being late. In all likelihood, you'll find there are no repercussions and as a result, you'll be much more inclined to do the same thing again next time. Likewise, just try not updating your website for a week and see if it hurts your traffic all that much. Again, probably fine, isn't it?

Your Personal Life

Most of what we've discussed so far has revolved around designing your work to avoid it interfering with your personal life. But for this to be effective it has to work both ways and you have to make sure that your personal life isn't interfering with work. That in turn, means that you have to be strict when it comes to not taking

Finding the CEO in You

calls, or meeting with friends during the hours of 9-5. And just as you put your work phone in a drawer in the evenings, you should consider putting your home phone in a drawer while you're working.

Of course you might decide you want to take advantage of your freedom by seeing friends more. In fact, meeting your friends on their lunch breaks can be a good way to avoid that cabin fever feeling and is always appreciated.

Or maybe you want to work in the morning and then again in the evening so you can spend the afternoon with family. Just make sure that this is pre-planned and that you have a strict cut off point for when your break ends and be consistent with that.

You can obviously give yourself the day off as well if you want to accept an exciting invitation but realize that this is a bigger commitment than it seems. You'll have to make that work up elsewhere and then it will be hard to get back into your routine. Moreover, if you bend your rules a few times, people will expect you to do it all the time. While it might not feel like it, being a bit strict and unsociable in the short term will actually allow you to spend more time with friends in the long.

~Thoughts~

Are you Happy

Chapter 25
Optimizing Performance, Health and Productivity

Now you have optimized your work/life balance and put systems and parameters in place to define your work hours, you should right away find that you have a lot more time and a lot more energy for working. You should be less stressed, a little less bipolar and a lot less tired.

Finding the CEO in You

This is the framework that will now allow you to build a truly healthy and optimal lifestyle. What you need to recognize is that your performance at work and your general health are intimately tied together. The happier and healthier you are during your time off, the better you will perform when you are working. The better you work, the more time you will have to focus on your own health.

And it all starts with sleep...

Optimizing Sleep

By employing a little strict discipline, you will find that you less often allow your work life to ruin your sleep. This is crucial because your output will be significantly neutered if you don't.

At the same time, you also need to make sure that you are doing everything else in your power to make sure your sleep is the best it can be.

For starters, this means going to bed at the same time every night and aiming to get a full 8 hours sleep. Again, this is sacred and it will make all the difference to every other aspect of your life. Going to bed at a strict time is what will help you set your internal rhythms, while waking up at the same time will prevent sleep inertia (and likewise prevent you from sleeping through your working morning).

Make sure that your room is pitch dark and that light is kept to an absolute minimum. Tape over the LEDs in the room and use heavy curtains to block out sunlight. Remember, you want to avoid 'blue light' so don't look at your phone or computer past 8pm. Caffeine should also be avoided after 4pm and note that alcohol can ruin the restorative nature of your rest.

A warm shower just before bed can also make a big difference to your sleep, as can stretching and perhaps practicing a little quiet meditation (meditation is also a great tool for encouraging mental discipline so that you aren't thinking about work). Make sure you get plenty of exercise and fresh air during the day too, so that you will be more tired when it comes to the evening.

Finally, nutrition is also critical for healthy sleep and specifically you need to be consuming enough vitamin D, magnesium, zinc and tryptophan to really maximize your deep sleep.

Exercise

Exercise is also a very important tool for the self-employed. Remember, working from home means you have no commute which means less exercise. At the same time, that means you have at least an hour you can commit to going to the gym in the morning and this will also help to boost your brain power.

Exercise triggers the release of BDNF – brain derived neurotrophic factor – which in turn increases learning, plasticity and attention. It also helps you get more blood to your brain and improves your mood and focus. All these things are great tools for boosting your performance and for combating health complaints.

Particularly important as well is stretching. Stretching also boosts IQ and at the same time it can prevent the mobility issues that come from working at a computer. Yoga is a particularly good practice but you can benefit simply from doing some stretches on a mat prior to lifting weights or doing CV.

Now you might have a desire to look like Arnold Schwarzenegger in which case, you need an entirely different book. But for the purposes of optimal productivity and health, you don't need to go mad in the gym. In fact, it's better that you don't. Instead, focus on exercise that will be enjoyable and that you'll be likely to stick to. Your whole aim here is to move regularly and to apply a little bit of positive stress (eustress) to your body to wake it up and strengthen it. Bodyweight training is particularly good for this, as is running.

Finding the CEO in You

Ultimately, remember that it's better to have a very easy training regime that you actually stick to, than an intense one that you never do…

And in this vein, it's also pertinent to find a gym that is near to you, or to set up your own home gym. If the gym is 10 miles away and requires driving, then it will eat into your day and your available energy levels.

~Thoughts~

_____
_____
_____
_____
_____
_____
_____
_____

Are you Happy

Finding the CEO in You

THE 15-MINUTE HOT ABS WORKOUT

Do the following moves up to three days a week, moving from one to the next with as little rest as possible after each. (You can rest for up to 60 seconds between circuits.) Repeat for a total of three circuits.

1 REVERSE WOOD CHOP
DO 5 REPS, THEN SWITCH SIDES

2 REVERSE LUNGE ROTATE
DO 5 REPS, THEN SWITCH SIDES

3 FOLDING CHAIR
DO 10 REPS

4 RULER REACH
DO 5 REPS, THEN SWITCH SIDES

Women'sHealth

Are you Happy

THE 15-MINUTE ANYTIME, ANYWHERE WORKOUT

Complete the exercises as instructed, moving from one to the next with little or no rest in between. Stop for 30 to 60 seconds at the end (if needed), then repeat the sequence up to two more times.

1 LEG CURL
DO 15 REPS

2 SEATED OBLIQUE TWIST
DO 20 REPS

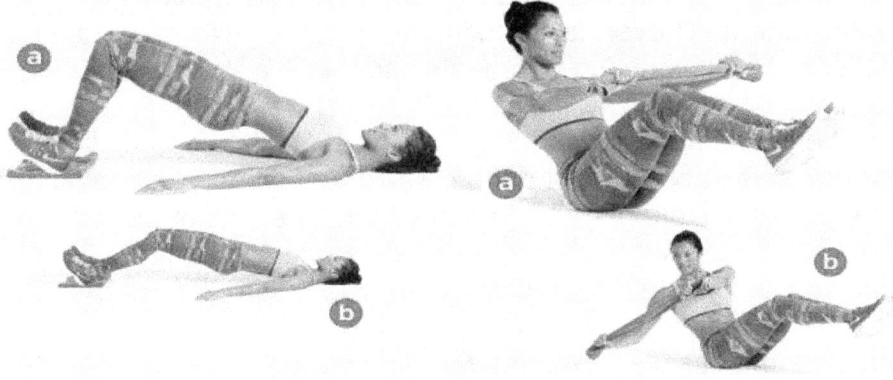

3 LATERAL LUNGE
DO 15 REPS, THEN SWITCH SIDES

4 SUPERMAN PRESS
DO 20 REPS

www.Body-workouts.com

Finding the CEO in You

Nutrition

This is the most important point of all: getting your nutrition right.

Again, our goal here is not to turn you into Superman or to give you gigantic pecs. Instead, the objective is to make you generally healthy, happy and able to work well. Avoiding obesity is part of that, so you do want to cut down on your carbs. Likewise, you want to avoid carbs and sugars because they can make you tired after your blood sugar has spiked.

Instead, focus on filling up with complex carbs, fats and proteins and don't overeat. Working from home means you can eat smaller snacks instead of big meals and this is also advisable.

The most important thing to remember of all though, is that your diet should be nutrient dense. This means that you should focus on getting lots of fruits, lots of vegetables, lots of meats and more. The benefits that zinc, potassium, sodium, vitamin C, B complex vitamins, lutein, calcium, l-tyrosine, l-carnitine, vitamin D, iron, omega 3 fatty acid, CoQ10, MCT oils and more have on your body cannot possibly be overstated. If you are getting your RDA of all these things, you will sleep better, feel happier, be thinner, think faster, be stronger… and the effects are more profound than any 'nootropic' or 'health supplement'. The best way to do this is just to eat lots of berries, fish, fruits, leafy greens, meats, organ meats and more.

Don't cut anything out your diet and do everything you can to give your body a varied and comprehensive selection of nutrients.

Are you Happy

Test Your Knowledge

1. The result of poor diet, generally caused by a lack of nutrients.   **A.** Vegetarian

2. The study of the nutrients in food and how they nourish the body.   **B.** Peak

3. Compounds produced by plants.   **C.** Lipid

4. How many basic categories of nutrients are there.   **D.** Soda

5. First in First out   **E.** Oxidation

6. Kosher salt has a _____ flavor than table salt and is somewhat coarser   **F.** Oils

7. A person that consumes no meat, fish or poultry products.   **G.** Fiber

8. A main source of energy for the body and are needed by the body to utilize protein and fat efficiently   **H.** Calories

9. Unique because it is on found in plant based food and cannot be digested by people   **I.** Raw

10. Often called "bad" cholesterol and is a result of eating foods with high levels of saturated fats and trans fats.   **J.** Organic

11. Eating ____ foods, especially fruits and vegetables, can provide nutritious options, but some foods provide more nutrients after cooking.   **K.** Nutrition

12. There are are several ways you can make a food more healthy including adding more fiber, fruits or vegetables,   **L.** Phytochemicals

or reducing _____

13. Products that have been grown without the use of pesticides or synthetic fertilizers.   **M.** Hormones

14. May provide additional nutritional value or may be more disease-resistant.   **N.** Genetically modified food

15. Without proper nutrition it is impossible for the human body to function at it's _____.   **O.** LDL

16. These fats are generally more saturated then liquid vegetable oils.   **P.** Fat content

17. This very important simple sugar is the body's primary source of energy.   **Q.** Six

18. A common starch   **R.** Potato

19. Are liquid at room temperature   **S.** Corn

20. An important hormone to regulate sugar is   **T.** Glucose

21. Another word for fat.   **U.** FIFO

22. The energy released by some nutrients is measured in   **V.** Carbohydrates

23. An example of a complex carbohydrate   **W.** purer

24. The chemical processes that causes unsaturated fats to spoil is called   **X.** Animal

25. special chemical messengers that regulate different body functions.   **Y.** Insulin

26. An example of a simple carbohydrate   **Z.** Malnutrition

Are you Happy

Introducing Kaizen

All this might sound like a lot to take on all at once, but if you're creating a business plan that supports these changes you'll find it's much easier. The changes you make to improve your health and energy will feed into your work life and the improved work life will feed into better health and energy – it's a virtuous cycle and that's why it makes sense to change everything at once, instead of viewing your 'diet' or your 'fitness' as isolated matters.

But if it's still sounding daunting, consider the concept of kaizen. Kaizen means making a small change in your lifestyle that will have ripples
affecting every other area. If you can't commit to changing your diet right away, instead just try committing to having a smoothie instead of a cappuccino first thing in the morning. Or commit to just doing 20 press ups in the evening.

This one change will likely be the beginning of huge repercussions in your life that lead to the healthy, happy, entrepreneurial you that you want to become.

~Thoughts~

_____
_____
_____
_____
_____
_____
_____
_____

Chapter 26
Home Business Models

Now you know how to manage your time, your energy, your workload and your clients and you should be happier, healthier and more productive as a result. You're finally putting your lifestyle first and your career second and that's what working from home should really be all about.

But none of this will be much use if you don't already work from home. So if you're still working in an office and now really keen to start out on your own, this section is for you. What's more, this section should also show you how you can set up more side-projects, or how you can adapt your current business model into something more conducive to a healthy lifestyle.

With that in mind then, here are some basic business models to consider…

Top Home Business Models for Lifestyle Design

Services

If you want to work on a computer, there are hundreds of different services you can provide online that are in high demand these days. Popular choices include web design, programming, graphic design, photography, copywriting and marketing.

Are you Happy

But there are others too: for instance, you can offer proof reading services, virtual assistant services, consultation, legal advice, publishing, product design, social media management and tons more. You could even become a talent agent – most jobs these days can be performed online in fact.

To start this business, all you need is to place an advert somewhere or respond to an advert. There are lots of places online that make this easy. Warrior Forum or Digital Point Forums for instance are forums frequented by website owners and digital marketers and you should be able to find lots of work here. Likewise, you can also find work by posting on outsourcing sites like Elance and UpWork. People Per Hour is another good one and you can also try simply calling or e-mailing business owners – or handing out business cards and going into stores!

This kind of work has the advantage of being straightforward – you get paid for the work you do. At the same time though, it's also a lot less scalable
and it's certainly not passive. It also means you'll be somewhat tied to the schedule of those you're working for.

Publishing

You can make money as a website owner, blogger, YouTube vlogger or any other kind of online publisher. To do so, you just have to build the popularity of your website and add AdSense (pay per click advertising), find a sponsor or sell a product (either of your own, or for commission).

All these systems work and they're very good at bringing in passive income. The only downside is that you have to put in the work in the first place and it can take a while to start seeing returns. A good compromise stance is to try earning money form a service, while using this time to gradually build a site.

Selling Products

Finding the CEO in You

You can sell products for commission (called affiliate marketing), you can sell e-books from your website, you can sell an app or you can sell products you buy.

To do the latter, all you need to do is find a cheap way to buy items in wholesale. Find a wholesaler or look on eBay and then order your t-shirts, CDs or whatever else it is you want to sell in a bulk. If you get about 100 to start with, it won't cost you too much and then of course you can sell them on for more than you paid for each one individually.

You can do this through your own website again but you don't need to – just as easily, you can start selling your product through eBay or through a landing page. Once you sell off the hundred you bought, you can then reinvest the profit into 200 more and gradually grow until you're making a big turnover. Note of course that you will need somewhere to store the items.

Section Thoughts:

This all sounds well and good but there's a good chance you won't go for any of these models. Why? Because you're too scared to give up your day job.

The good news for you then is that you don't have to. In fact, the much better way to make this work is to start with a small business and slowly grow it in your free time (as a hobby) and then to quit your job only when you have enough work.

Take two weeks off work for instance and try finding some clients to do marketing for. If you find them easily enough and they seem to be offering steady work… then you can hand in your notice.

Or start building a website on your lunch break and at weekends – it should be fun and something you enjoy anyway. If it starts making money, then you can maybe work less and eventually quit altogether.

Are you Happy

Do bear in mind that you need to approach this plan seriously if you want it to work. If you really want to start earning a living from home, then don't come up with some elaborate plan to make the next Facebook. That might work, sure, but it's not a very reliable short term strategy for improving your lifestyle. There's no need to reinvent the wheel here – just go with a business model that has been proven to work and then execute it flawlessly.

And most of all make sure that when you do this, you also think about the lifestyle you want and how that business is going to help you get that lifestyle. Think about your health, think about your sleep and think about your stress levels. Is your business model designed to support the life you want, or are you still stuck in reverse?

~Thoughts~

_____
_____
_____
_____
_____
_____
_____
_____
_____
_____
_____
_____
_____
_____
_____
_____

Finding the CEO in You

Take Home Lessons

- Build a business plan that focuses on lifestyle first

- Remember that 'success' doesn't always lead to that lifestyle you want...

- Trial your business while you're still working and quit when it works

- There's no need to reinvent the wheel!

- Don't work in your living room, make the most of your freedom

- If you don't want to be a digital nomad, you can still take more holidays and travel in short bursts!

- Be strict and disciplined with your working hours, your social time and bed time

- Sleep is sacred!

- Eat a healthy diet full of vitamins and nutrients

- Separate your work-life and home-life by using different devices, auto responders and virtual assistants

- Make a pact with an entrepreneurial friend to help each other out in a crisis

Are you Happy

- Try not to stress too much if you are forced to hand in work a little late

- Have multiple revenue streams

Business Plan Template found on www.template.net

[Your Company Logo]
[Your Company Name]

[Type of Business] Business Plan

[Date Submitted]

Prepared By
[Name]
[Job Title]
[Phone]
[Email]

Executive Summary

Provide a summary of the whole document, narrating a short overview of the company, its structure, founder/s, founding date, and core team members. State the nature of the business, its target market, and the value it provides its clients.

Include the sales, marketing, operational, and financial plans of the company. Describe how the business can achieve growth with these strategies.

Lastly, mention the company's direct and indirect competition and its competitive advantages over its competitors.

Company Overview

Mission Statement
State, in a concise manner, the overall aims of the company and the core reason for its existence.

Philosophy
The philosophy statement pertains to the way things are done around your organization. It consists of the core values, beliefs, and ethics that guide the actions and decision-making processes of the people in your business.

Vision
Briefly state the long-term aspirations of the company upon achieving its goals and objectives.

Outlook
Describe the market or economic outlook that has a profound impact on information technology (IT) businesses. This could be the robust growth of the population in the area, the increase in the gross domestic product of your state, or the accumulation of competing companies in your city, or other factors. Describe the state of the particular market niche of the business and the professional forecast about it.

Are you Happy

Type of Industry

State the type of industry that the company will operate in.

Business Structure & Ownership
Describe the business structure and ownership of the IT company.

Services

Description
Provide a detailed description of each of the IT services the company is offering.

Value Proposition
Describe the value of the company offers its customers in terms of services, expertise, flexibility, speed, cost-efficiency, transparency, etc. Be as concise as possible.

Marketing Analysis

Industry Overview and Trends
Provide a short narrative of the IT industry's market and economic status. Cite emerging trends that could possibly impact the company as well as the industry at large. You may use graphs and tables to present information that is relevant to this section.

Target Market
Expound on what market population is the main target for your IT services.

Market Size
Present the potential size of your target market per draw area. You may create your own table according to the specifications of your target market and services.

Draw Area	Size	% of Total

Finding the CEO in You

Total		

Market Segmentation

Describe the target population of the business according to the following market characteristics:

Demographic	Behavioral
- - - - -	- - - -
Psychographic	**Geographic**
- - -	- - -

SWOT Analysis

Determine the IT company's strengths, weaknesses, opportunities, and threats using the table below.

Are you Happy

Strengths - Processes - Resources - Skills, Talents, and Knowledge - Assets - Competitive advantage	**Opportunities** - Market trends - Consumer behavior - Events - Government regulation and policies - Technology
Weaknesses - Improvements needed - Errors - Factors that are lacking	**Threats** - Competitors - Supply and demand - Market and consumer trends - Consumer behavior - Technology - Government regulation and policy

Competition
State the organization's direct and indirect competitors.

Direct and Indirect Competition

[Company Name]	Direct Competition	Indirect Competition
Mention the type of services you are offering.	Mention the name of your direct competitor.	Mention the name of your indirect competitor.

Competitive Analysis

	Strength	Weakness	Opportunity	Threat

Finding the CEO in You

[Company Name]	Internal or specific to the company	Internal or specific to the company	An external factor that provides a business opportunity to the industry in general or something specific within the company.	An external factor that threatens the success of the industry in general or something specific within the company.
[Direct Competitor]				
[Indirect Competitor]				

Marketing Plan

Provide a concise statement of the company's plans to market its services based on the data and information analyzed through the SWOT and competitive analyses.

[Marketing activity]
Provide a detailed description of the marketing activity.

[Marketing activity]
Provide a detailed description of the marketing activity.

Are you Happy

[Marketing activity]
Provide a detailed description of the marketing activity.

[Marketing activity]
Provide a detailed description of the marketing activity.

[Marketing activity]
Provide a detailed description of the marketing activity.

Marketing Strategy

List down the company's marketing strategies along with each of its specific activities, timeline, and success criteria.

Marketing Strategy 1	[Marketing activity]
Activities	
Timeline	
Success Criteria	

Finding the CEO in You

Marketing Strategy 2	[Marketing activity]
Activities	
Timeline	
Success Criteria	

Marketing Strategy 3	[Marketing activity]
Activities	
Timeline	
Success Criteria	

Marketing Strategy 4	[Marketing activity]
Activities	
Timeline	

	Are you Happy
Success Criteria	

Marketing Strategy 5	[Marketing activity]	
Activities		
Timeline		
Success Criteria		

Pricing Strategy

Note how the IT company prices its services for its clients. Pricing strategies can be cost-plus pricing, premium pricing, penetration pricing, or project-based pricing. Provide a brief description of the chosen strategy.

Operational Plan

Operating Hours

Detail the company's hours of operation. Mention how many hours a day it operates and for how many days a week. You may also include the opening and closing time. Also, note if the company will be operating during major holidays, such as Christmas, the Fourth of July, and Thanksgiving.

Location

Provide a detailed description of the company's location. Describe the building and its surrounding area and explain why that location has been chosen as the main office for the IT business.

Location	Description

Finding the CEO in You

Immediate Area	
Type of Area	
Adjacent Uses	
Benefits	
Proximity	
Customer Type	
Size of Potential Customers	
Competitors	
Traffic Volume	
Patterns	
Pedestrians	
Periods	
Accessibility	
Proximity to Major Streets	
Entrance/Exit	
Visibility	

Are you Happy

View From the Road	
Exterior Appearance	
Landscaping	

Organizational Structure

Illustrate the company's organizational structure below. You may create a different structure that best fits your business.

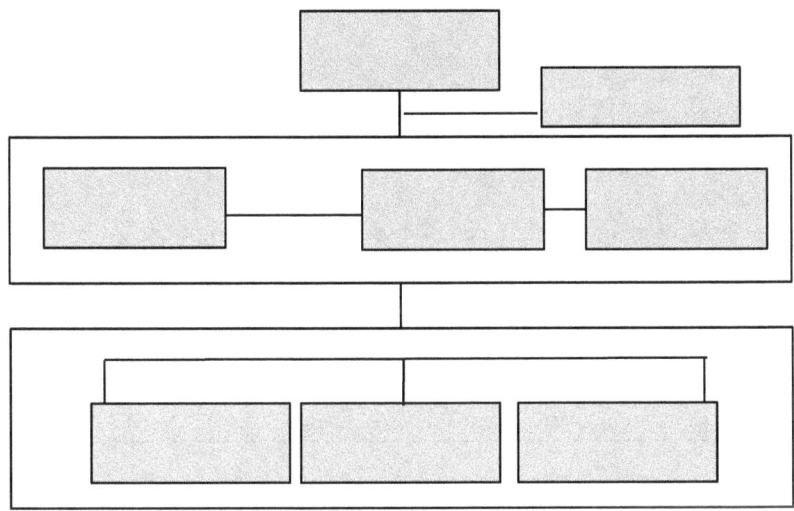

Key Staff

List down the key employees of the company together with their position and other information relevant to their employment to the company.

Name	[Name of Staff]	[Name of Staff]	[Name of Staff]

Finding the CEO in You

Position	[Role]	[Role]	[Role]
Date Joined	[Date]	[Date]	[Date]
Experience	[Expertise]	[Expertise]	[Expertise]
Highest Qualification	[Qualification]	[Qualification]	[Qualification]
Salary	[Salary]	[Salary]	[Salary]

Financial Plan

Assumptions

Provide a brief statement of the IT company's financial assumptions. Also, mention the cost of the start-up and the source of the money.

You may use the sample table formats provided below, or you may use a different format that fits your organization better.

[Your Company Name]				
Business Start-Up Costs in USD				
FUNDING			**Estimated**	**Actual**	**Over/(Under)**

Are you Happy

Investor Funding				
	Owner 1			
	Owner 2			
	Other			
	Total Investment			
Loans				
	Bank Loan 1			
	Bank Loan 2			
	Non-Bank Loan 1			
	Total Loans			
Other Funding				
	Grant 1			

Finding the CEO in You

		Estimated	Actual	Under/(Over)
	Other			
	Total Other Funding			
TOTAL FUNDING		0.00	0.00	0.00
COSTS		Estimated	Actual	Under/(Over)
Fixed Costs				
	Advertising for Opening			
	Basic Website			
	Brand Development			
	Building Down Payment			
	Building Improvements/Remodeling			
	Business Cards/Stationery			

Are you Happy

Business Entity	
Business Licenses/Permits	
Computer Hardware/Software	
Decorating	
Franchise Start-Up Fees	
Internet Setup Deposit	
Lease Security Deposit	
Legal/Professional Fees	
Machines & Equipment	
Office Furniture/Fixtures	
Operating Cash (Working Capital)	
Point of Sale Hardware/Software	
Prepaid Insurance	

Finding the CEO in You

Public Utility Deposits			
Reserve for Contingencies			
Security System Installation			
Setup, Installation and Consulting fees			
Signage			
Starting Inventory			
Telephone			
Tools & Supplies			
Travel			
Truck & Vehicle			
Other 1 (specify)			
Other 2 (specify)			
Total Fixed Costs	0.00	0.00	0.00

Are you Happy

Average Monthly Costs

- Advertising (print, broadcast and Internet)
- Business Insurance
- Business Vehicle Insurance
- Employee Salaries and Commissions
- Equipment Lease Payments
- Inventory, Raw Materials, Parts
- Franchise Fee
- Health Insurance
- Internet Connection
- Loan and Credit Card Interest & Principal
- Legal/Accounting Fees
- Merchant Account Fees
- Miscellaneous Expenses
- Mortgage Payments

Finding the CEO in You

Lease Payment			
Owner Salary			
Payroll Taxes or Self-Employment Tax			
Postage/Shipping Costs			
Security System Monthly Payment			
Supplies			
Telephone			
Travel			
Public Utilities			
Website Hosting/Maintenance			
Other 1 (specify)			
Other 2 (specify)			
Total Average Monthly Costs	0.00	0.00	0.00
x Number of Months	12		
Total Monthly Costs	0.00	0.00	0.00

Are you Happy

TOTAL COSTS		0.00	0.00	0.00
SURPLUS/(DEFICIT)		0.00	0.00	0.00

The table below should depict the company's sales forecast for the first six months, containing details on its number of business transactions per draw area and their respective projects.

Draw Area	Month YEAR	Month YEAR	Month YEAR	Month YEAR	Month YEAR	Month YEAR	Total
[Area]							
[Area]							
[Area]							
[Area]							
Subtotal							

Finding the CEO in You

Statements

Income Statement

[Your Company Name]

Income Statement

For the Year Ended [Date]

Gross Project Revenues	0
Direct Project Costs on Contracts	
Depreciation of Equipment	
Estimating	
Administrative and Other Expenses	
Subtotal of Costs and Expenses	0
Operating Income	0
Interest Expense	
Income Before Taxes	0
Tax Expense	
Income After Tax	0

Are you Happy

Cash Dividends	
Net Income/Retained Earnings	0
Retained Earnings, Beginning	
Retained Earnings at End of Year	$0.00

Profit and Loss Projection

[Your Company Name]
Profit and Loss (in USD)
For the Year Ended [Date]

	FY[YEAR]	%	FY[YEAR]	%
SALES				
Revenue - Services	0.00	0%	0.00	0%
Total Sales	**0.00**	**0%**	**0.00**	**0%**
COST OF SALES				
Cost of Contract - Labor	0.00	0%	0.00	0%
Cost of Contract - Materials	0.00	0%	0.00	0%
Cost of Contract - Equipment	0.00	0%	0.00	0%

Finding the CEO in You

Cost of Contract - Others	0.00	0%	0.00	0%
Total Cost of Sales	**0.00**	**0%**	**0.00**	**0%**
GROSS PROFIT (Total Sales - Total Cost of Sales)	**0.00**	**0%**	**0.00**	**0%**
INDIRECT EXPENSES				
Salaries and wages - Vacation, Holiday, etc.	0.00	0%	0.00	0%
Salaries and wages - Salary, Bonus, and Benefits	0.00	0%	0.00	0%
Payroll Tax	0.00	0%	0.00	0%
Insurance - Workers' Compensation	0.00	0%	0.00	0%
401(k) Employer Portion	0.00	0%	0.00	0%
Insurance - Health and Dental	0.00	0%	0.00	0%
Employee Tool Allowance	0.00	0%	0.00	0%
Equipment Parts	0.00	0%	0.00	0%
Equipment Depreciation	0.00	0%	0.00	0%
Interest and taxes	0.00	0%	0.00	0%
Indirect Labor Cost	0.00	0%	0.00	0%
Equipment Applied Cost	0.00	0%	0.00	0%
Total Indirect Expenses	**0.00**	**0%**	**0.00**	**0%**

Are you Happy

GENERAL AND ADMINISTRATIVE EXPENSES				
Wages and Salaries - Admin	0.00	0%	0.00	0%
Commission - Sales	0.00	0%	0.00	0%
Payroll Tax	0.00	0%	0.00	0%
Insurance - Workers' Compensation	0.00	0%	0.00	0%
401 (k) Employer Portion	0.00	0%	0.00	0%
Insurance - Health and Dental	0.00	0%	0.00	0%
Office Supplies	0.00	0%	0.00	0%
Utilities	0.00	0%	0.00	0%
Telephone	0.00	0%	0.00	0%
Licenses, Permits, and Fees	0.00	0%	0.00	0%
Total General and Administrative Expenses	**0.00**	**0%**	**0.00**	**0%**
NET INCOME	0.00		0.00	
Profit Margin*	0.00		0.00	
***Not part of P&L**				

Finding the CEO in You

Balance Sheet Projection

	[Your Company Name]	
	Balance Sheet (in USD)	
	[Date of Coverage]	
	ASSETS	
CURRENT ASSETS	YEAR	YEAR
Cash and Cash Equivalents	0.00	
Accounts Receivable		
Allowance for Doubtful Accounts		
Accounts Receivable, net of allowance for doubtful accounts		
Retainage		
Other		
Inventory		
Cost in Excess of Billings		
Deferred Tax Asset		
Prepaid Expenses		

Are you Happy

Total Current Assets	0.00	0.00

FIXED ASSETS

Property, Land, Building		
Equipment and Vehicles		
Subtotal	0.00	0.00
Less: Accumulated Depreciation		
Total Fixed Assets	0.00	0.00

INTANGIBLE ASSETS

Trademarks and Patents		
Goodwill		
Total Intangible Assets	0.00	0.00
Total Assets	0.00	0.00

LIABILITIES AND SHAREHOLDER'S EQUITY

Finding the CEO in You

CURRENT LIABILITIES

Accounts Payable	0.00	
Accrued Expenses/Deferred Income		
Loans Payable		
Notes Payable		
Other Short-Term Payable		
Total Current Liabilities	**0.00**	**0.00**

NONCURRENT LIABILITIES

Long-Term Debt		
Others		
Total Noncurrent Liabilities	**0.00**	**0.00**

TOTAL LIABILITIES	**0.00**	**0.00**

SHAREHOLDER'S EQUITY

Invested Capital

Are you Happy

Retained Earnings		
TOTAL SHAREHOLDER'S EQUITY	0.00	0.00
TOTAL LIABILITIES & EQUITY	0.00	0.00

Cash Flow Projection

[Your Company Name]	
Cash Flow	
As of [Date]	
Cash Flow from Operating Activities	
Cash flow received from customers	0.00
Wages and salaries	
Payments to suppliers and vendors	0.00
Paid Interest	
Paid Tax	
Cash generated from operations	
Net Cash from Operating Activities	0.00

Finding the CEO in You

Cash Flow from Investing Activities	
Purchase of land, property, and equipment	0.00
Proceeds from the sale of equipment	
Net Cash Used in Investing Activities	0.00
Cash Flow from Financing Activities	
Proceeds from common stock	
Payment to long-term debt	0.00
Paid dividends	
Net Cash Used in Financing Activities	0.00
Net Increase (Decrease) in Cash	0.00
Cash Balance January	0.00
Cash and Cash Equivalents at the End of Period	0.00

Are you Happy

Part IV
The Expert In You

Are you Happy

Self esteem is important. Feeling good about who you are and having confidence in yourself is something everyone should do, but many don't. The problem often lies in that they try to do something when they're younger and fail at it. If it happens more than once, they begin to lose confidence in their abilities and too many times, never gain it back.

Often, self esteem keeps us from reaching our goals. If you don't feel good about yourself, you often don't realize things you're good at. When you're told negative things about yourself from childhood, it's hard to turn those feelings around. It's time you stop giving yourself a pity party. Open your eyes. Dig deep inside yourself and discover what it is that makes you special. You can do it!

How to Find Your Expertise

You may be saying, "You don't know me. I don't have anything I'm good at." You can say that until you're blue in the face, and I'll never believe it. Why? It's simple. I've been there and done that. I'd say at one point in our lives everyone has felt like they're not good at anything. It's time to get over that negative self-talk and move on to finding that talent that is buried within you.

There are several ways to find out what your expertise is. Of course, if your opinion is that you can't do anything, don't rely on yourself for impartial judgment on that. You are, however, a good place to start.

Will you be good at everything you try…of course not! No one is good at everything. You can find what you are good at though. Maybe you love the theater. You may have a life-time dream of

Are you Happy

being an actor/actress. The problem is…you can't act. Acting is a talent. You either have it or you don't. Sometimes you can take every class or training course there is in a subject, and know that you'll never be more than mediocre at it. Does that mean you still can't work doing something you love? NO—you just have to look at the alternatives.

Maybe you're a good organizer and planner. Maybe that dream you have of being an actor/actress gives you a vision. Instead of wasting money on acting lessons, you can train to be a director. If you like to like writing, maybe you can write scripts. Maybe you're a master builder and you can build stage sets. I'm sure you understand what I'm trying to tell you. Take what you're good at and work it into something you feel passionate about. Then, you'll enjoy your work. You'll be better at it, and feel better about yourself.

This book will help you discover what your talents are and teach you how to take those talents and monetize on them. Make money doing something you love.

What are you good at? Life doesn't come with instructions. There's no genie that's going to pop out of a bottle and tell you what you're good at. You have to figure that out for yourself. Often it's a process of trial and error. Ironically, we find out what we're good at many times by eliminating what we're not good at. We learn from our mistakes as much as we learn from our successes.

It's up to you to take the first step. You have to decide that you know you're good at something and start down the road to determining exactly what that something is. You have some skill that you're passionate about that you can turn into profit. It's time you set out to find it.

To begin the process of determining what you're good at, write everything down. Get a piece of paper and a pen and start writing down anything you do well. The key here is to not forget the little things. Everyone knows if they're good at big things, like the singing example used earlier, but the little things are often neglected. Are you a good listener? Do you work well with people? Are you an organizer? Are you good with numbers? Do you like planning things like parties? Are you compassionate toward others? Do you have a hobby you're good at? Maybe you're good with languages. The list is practically endless.

Maybe there's something on your current job that you've been told you're good at. Does your supervisor ask you to head committees? Have you never been short on your drawer if you're a cashier? Is everything cleaner when you do it? Maybe you're good at seeing the overall picture and spotting errors quickly in print or lists of numbers. I'm sure you've been told by your supervisor or a fellow employee that you're good at something, even if you didn't believe it at the time, write it down. In this particular step in the process, it doesn't matter if it's something you're passionate about.

Just tell if you're good at it. Don't shortchange yourself! Little things matter.

Don't just assume you can't answer this question immediately that you're not good at anything. If you can't identify things you're good at, write a list of everything you do each day, on and off the job. They go back and look at each one and if you don't have a problem doing it, then you're good at it so write it to the list. Ask someone you feel is a trusted friend for ideas. Often your friends know you better than you know yourself. Hey, I figure if my friends know me for who I am and love me anyway, I have to have a few good points, right? You do too. Let them help you get the list started.

Still stuck? If you are, your self-esteem is probably just too low to ever feel good about yourself and your abilities without proof that you're good at them. If that is the case, there are tests that you can take that will help you. There are three I'd recommend:

Learning Styles Preference Test—This can be done online or by using a paper/pencil version, and it takes about 5-10 minutes. If simply search on Google, you can find many different types that are free to take and give you at least the three basic learning types:

Auditory—Learn by hearing

Are you Happy

Visual—Learn by seeing
Tactile/Kinesthetic—Learn by using hand-on methods

This will begin by giving you a sense of why some things are easier for you than others. For example, if you're a tactile learner, you may be able to type very quickly, or take an engine apart and put it back together, but reading and answering questions can be a chore for you. You can do it, but it takes you longer than you feel it should. Others could do it quickly growing up, so you felt they were smarter than you.

Not so…many tactile learners have above-average IQ's, but never know it. Realizing how you learn will help you realize you're smart too, just in different ways.

Auditory learners are usually those that did well when classes were more of a lecture type class, and visual learners usually excelled when a lot of reading was involved. Each person can be equally intelligent, but if taught in a way they have difficulty learning, they might not grasp things as well. Simply by taking the preference test and looking at the questions will have you saying…I do that well. Oh, I do that too. It will begin giving you thing to write down.

Personality Test—What kind of person are you? One area on this type of tests simply lets you discover if you're an introvert or an extrovert? You probably have a good idea about that, but many people just think that means one is outgoing and the other is a homebody. Not true. This job gives you preferences of skills such as: Do you think, then act/act, then think? Are you comfortable when you're alone/prefer to be around a lot of people? Would you rather work behind the scenes/like taking a public role? These tests also give you a better feel for who you are. The questions will have you finding more and more things you didn't realize you were good at. Write them on the list. There are sites online that offer these types of tests free as well and they can be taken in a matter of minutes.

Finding the CEO in You

MYERS-BRIGGS TYPE INDICATOR
By Katharine C. Briggs & Isabel Briggs Myers

Directions:

There are no "right" or "wrong" answers to the questions on this inventory. Your answers will help to show how you like to look at things and how you like to go about deciding things. Knowing your own preferences and learning about other people's can help you understand whether your special strenghts are, what kind of work you might enjoy and be successful doing, and how people with different preferences can relate to each other and be valuable to society.

Read each question carefully and select one of the two choices given, which applies to you, by circling to either "A" or "B".

PART1: Which answer comes closer to telling how you usually feel or act?

1. WHEN YOU GO SOMEWHERE FOR THE DAY, WOULD YOU RATHER

    A. PLAN WHAT YOU WILL DO AND WHEN, OR

    B. JUST GO!!

2. IF YOU WERE A TEACHER, WOULD YOU RATHER TEACH

    A. FACTS-BASED COURSES, OR

    B. COURSES INVOLVING OPINION OR THEORY?

3. ARE YOU USUALLY

    A. A "GOOD MIXER" WITH GROUPS OF PEOPLE, OR

    B. RATHER QUIET AND RESERVED?

4. DO YOU MORE OFTEN LET

    A. YOUR HEART RULE YOUR HEAD. OR

    B. YOUR HEAD RULE YOUR HEART?

Are you Happy

5. IN DOING SOMETHING THAT MANY OTHER PEOPLE DO, WOULD YOU RATHER

    A. INVENT A WAY OF YOUR OWN, OR

    B. DO IT IN THE ACCEPTED WAY?

6. AMONG YOUR FRIENDS ARE YOU

    A. FULL OF NEWS ABOUT EVERYBODY, OR

    B. ONE OF THE LAST TO HEAR WHAT IS GOING ON?

7. DOES THE IDEA OF MAKING A LIST OF WHAT YOU SHOULD GET DONE OVER A WEEKEND

    A. HELP YOU, OR

    B. STRESS YOU, OR

    C. POSITIVELY DEPRESS YOU?

8. WHEN YOU HAVE A SPECIAL JOB TO DO, DO YOU LIKE TO

    A. ORGANIZE IT CAREFULLY BEFORE YOU START, OR

    B. FIND OUT WHAT IS NECESSARY AS YOU GO ALONG?

9. DO YOU TEND TO HAVE

    A. BROAD FRIENDSHIPS WITH MANY DIFFERENT PEOPLE, OR

    B. DEEP FRIENDSHIP WITH VERY FEW PEOPLE?

10. DO YOU ADMIRE MORE THE PEOPLE WHO ARE

    A. NORMAL-ACTING TO NEVER MAKE THEMSELVES THE CENTER OF ATTENTION, OR

    B. TOO ORIGINAL AND INDIVIDUAL TO CARE WHETHER THEY ARE THE CENTER OF ATTENTION OR NOT

11. DO YOU PREFER TO

    A. ARRANGE PICNICS, PARTIES ETC, WELL IN ADVANCE, OR

    B. BE FREE TO DO WHATEVER TO LOOKS LIKE FUN WHEN THE TIME COMES?

12. DO YOU USUALLY GET ALONG BETTER WITH

    A. REALISTIC PEOPLE, OR

    B. IMAGINATIVE PEOPLE?

13. WHEN YOU ARE WITH THE GROUP OF PEOPLE, WOULD YOU USUALLY RATHER

    A. JOIN IN THE TALK OF THE GROUP OR

    B. STAND BACK AND LISTEN FIRST?

14. IS IT A HIGHER COMPLIMENT TO BE CALLED

    A. A PERSON OF REAL FEELING, OR

    B. A CONSISTENTLY REASONABLE PERSON?

15. IN READING FOR PLEASURE, DO YOU

    A. ENJOY ODD OR ORIGINAL WAYS OF SAYING THINGS, OR

    B. LIKE WRITERS TO SAY EXACTLY WHAT THEY MEAN?

16. DO YOU

    A. TALK EASILY TO ALMOST ANYONE FOR AS LONG AS YOU HAVE TO, OR

    B. FIND A LOT TO SAY ONLY TO CERTAIN PEOPLE OR UNDER CERTAIN CONDITIONS?

17. DOES FOLLOWING A SCHEDULE

    A. APPEAL TO YOU, OR
    B. CRAMP YOU?

Are you Happy

18. WHEN IT IS SETTLED WELL IN ADVANCE THAT YOU WILL DO A CERTAIN THING AT A CERTAIN TIME, DO YOU FIND IT

    A. NICE TO BE ABLE TO PLAN ACCORDINGLY, OR

    B. A LITTLE UNPLEASANT TO BE TIED DOWN?

19. ARE YOU MORE SUCCESSFUL

    A. AT FOLLOWING A CAREFULLY WORKED OUT PLAN, OR

    B. AT DEALING WITH THE UNEXPECTED AND SEEING QUICKLY WHAT SHOULD BE DONE?

20. WOULD YOU RATHER BE CONSIDERED

    A. A PRACTICAL PERSON, OR

    B. AN OUT-OF-THE-BOX-THINKING PERSON?

21. IN A LARGE GROUP, DO YOU MORE OFTEN

    A. INTRODUCE OTHERS, OR

    B. GET INTRODUCED?

22. DO YOU USUALLY

    A. VALUE EMOTION MORE THAN LOGIC, OR

    B. VALUE LOGIC MORE THAN FEELINGS?

23. WOULD YOU RATHER HAVE AS A FRIEND

    A. SOMEONE WHO IS ALWAYS COMING UP WITH NEW IDEAS, OR

    B. SOMEONE WHO HAS BOTH FEET ON THE GROUND?

Finding the CEO in You

24. CAN THE NEW PEOPLE YOU MEET TELL WHAT YOU ARE INTERESTED IN

    A. RIGHT AWAY,
    B. ONLY AFTER THEY REALLY GET TO KNOW YOU?

25. (ON THIS QUESTION ONLY, IF TWO ANSWERS ARE TRUE, CIRCLE BOTH)
    IN YOUR DAILY WORK, DO YOU

    A. USUALLY PLAN YOUR WORK SO YOU WON'T NEED TO WORK UNDER PRESSURE, OR
    B. RATHER ENJOY AN EMERGENCY THAT MAKES YOU WORK AGAINST TIME, OR
    C. HATE TO WORK UNDER PRESSURE?

26. DO YOU USUALLY

    A. SHOW YOUR FEELINGS FREELY, OR
    B. KEEP YOUR FEELINGS TO YOURSELF?

Part 2: Which word in each pair appeals to you more?
(Think what the word means, not how they look or how they sound)

27. A. SCHEDULED B. UNPLANNED	35. A. STATEMENT B. CONCEPT	43. A. CALM B. LIVELY
28. A. FACTS B. IDEAS	36. A. RESERVED B. TALAKATIVE	44. A. JUSTICE B. MERCY
29. A. QUIET B. HEARTY	37. A. ANALYZE B. SYMPATHIZE	45. A. FASCINATING B. SENSIBLE
30. A. CONVINCING B. TOUCHING	38. A. CREATE B. MAKE	46. A. FIRM-MINDED B. WARM HEARTED
31. A. IMAGINATIVE B. MATTER-OF-FACT	39. A. DETERMINED B. DEVOTED	47. A. FEELING B. THINKING
32. A. BENEFITS B. BLESSINGS	40. A. GENTLE B. FIRM	48. A. LITERAL B. FIGURATIVE

Are you Happy

33. A. PEACEMAKER
    B. JUDGE

34. A. SYSTEMATIC
    B. SPONTANEOUS

41. A. SYSTEMATIC
    B. CASUAL

42. A. CERTAINTY
    B. THEORY

49. A. ANTICIPATION
    B. COMPASSION

50. A. HARD
    B. SOFT

M.B.T.I SCORING SHEET

DIRECTIONS:

Circle the question number with your corresponding choice. (For example: If you chose "A" for question 1., then circle "1A" under the **J** category. Note: the questions are listed under the letter category for which they correspond and are therefore out of order.)

After you have circled your choices to each of the questions, add up the points for each of your circled choices within each category. (For example: if you circled 3A, 9A, 13A, 16A, and 36B under the **E** category, your total points would be 2+2+1+2+2=9 points.)

E		I		S		N		T		F		J		P	
Q&C	P	Q&C	P	Q&C	P	Q&C	P	Q&C	P	Q&C	P	Q&C	P	Q&C	P
3A	2	3B	2	2A	2	2B	2	4B	2	4A	1	1A	2	1B	2
6A	2	6B	1	5B	1	5A	1	14B	2	14A	1	7A	1	7B	1
9A	2	9B	1	10A	1	10B	2	22B	2	22A	2			7C	1
13A	1	13B	2	12A	1	12B	2	30A	2	30B	1	8A	1	8B	2
16A	2	16B	2	15B	1	15A	0	32A	1	32B	1	11A	2	11B	1
21A	2	21B	2	20A	2	20B	2	33B	2	33A	0	17A	2	17B	2
24A	1	24B	1	23B	2	23A	1	37A	1	37B	2	18A	1	18B	1
26A	1	26B	0	28A	2	28B	1	39A	1	39B	1	19A	1	19B	1
29B	2	29A	2	31B	2	31A	0	40B	2	40A	1	25A	1	25B	1
36B	2	36A	1	35A	2	35B	1	44A	1	44B	2	25C	0		
43B	1	43A	1	38B	2	38A	0	46A	2	46B	0	27A	2	27B	2
				42A	1	42B	2	47B	2	47A	1	34A	2	34B	2
				45B	2	45A	0	49A	2	49B	1	41A	2	41B	2
				48A	1	48B	1	50A	2	50B	0				
TOTAL POINTS		TOTAL POINTS		TOTAL POINTS		TOTAL POINTS		TOTAL POINTS		TOTAL POINTS		TOTAL POINTS		TOTAL POINTS	

LEGEND Q &C = QUESTION & CHOICE
P=POINTS

Finding the CEO in You

Compare your total points for **E** and **I**, **S** and **N**, **T** and **F**, and **J** and **P**. The letter with the greater points value is your peronality type. Put this letter in the corresponding box below:

MY PERSONALITY TYPE IS => | E/I | S/N | T/F | J/P |
|---|---|---|---|
| | | | |

IN CASE OF A TIE

1) between E & I, select I
2) between S & N, select N
3) between T & F, male will select 'T' & females 'F'
4) between J & P, select P

Personality traits explained:

Mind:

Introverted (I) – prefer solitary activities, think before speaking, get exhausted by social interaction.
Extraverted (E) – prefer group activities, think while speaking, get energized by social interaction.

Energy:

Intuitive (N) – imaginative, rely on their intuition, absorbed in ideas, focus on what might happen.
Sensing (S) – down-to-earth, rely on their senses, absorbed in practical matters, focus on what has happened.

Nature:

Thinking (T) - tough, follow their minds, focus on objectivity and rationality.
Feeling (F) – sensitive, follow their hearts, focus on harmony and cooperation.

Tactics:

Judging (J) – decisive, prefer clear rules and guidelines, see deadlines as sacred, seek closure.
Perceiving (P) – very good at improvising, prefer keeping their options open, relaxed about their work, seek freedom.

www.16personalities.com

Are you Happy

Career Assessment Test—These tests are a little more involved, and take a bit longer. One place you can get a good valid test is your state's version of the government unemployment office free of charge. Employment centers also give these kinds of tests, but sometimes there is a fee for them. If you're only going to take one test, this should be it. It's test questions are geared at asking you questions and showing you how even things you feel may be silly that you do well can lead to wise, enjoyable career choices

Instructions – Self-Assessment: Part 1

- Allow approximately 15 minutes to complete the Self-Assessment.
- Read through the list of Interests, Skills and Values and mark each one according to the options provided.
- When completing your self –assessment reflect on your previous jobs, your current role and the possibilities of future positions and opportunities.
- Please feel free to add additional interests, skills or values that apply to your specialist knowledge or expertise.

Instructions – Profile: Part 2

- Allow approximately 20 minutes to complete your profile.
- Part 2 of the exercise involves summarising the key findings from your self-assessment by completing the 'Profile' template attached.
- Review your responses from the self-assessment and begin by listing your top 10 interests, 10 of your strongest skills and top 10 values.
- List things you would like to do less of, skills acquired in the past you enjoy which are not currently utilised

(hidden talents) and list the top 10 skills you would like to learn.

- This profile is a valuable marketing tool, detailing a great deal of valuable information.
- If you identify more than 10 options for each section of the profile please add them. It is equality acceptable to list less than 10 options for each section if applicable.
- Complete the profile by listing any potential barriers and obstacles which you feel might affect your career development opportunities.

Are you Happy

Interest	Of great interest	Interested sometimes	Of no interest
Using your imagination and expressing ideas			
Problem solving			
Establishing systems and procedures			
Teaching and explaining			
Guiding and coaching			
Supervising others			
Making a difference in other people's lives			
Working with things rather than people			
Building, assembling, fixing and making things			
Being active rather than sitting			
Scheduling and monitoring			
Presenting information and ideas in creative ways			
Sales and marketing			
Focusing on customer service and service standards			
Visual arts, music and performing			
Sports and fitness			
Organising and setting priorities			
Managing physical resources or organising spaces			

Finding the CEO in You

Community service and human welfare			
Analysing and interpreting results			
Taking financial and business risks			
Administration tasks and processes			
Researching and examining ideas and theories			
Leading, directing and managing people			
Discovery and investigation, seeking solutions			
Applying logic and exploring abstract ideas			
Appreciation of design and style- decorating and designing			
Writing – articles, memos, stories, creative pieces			
Social media			

Interest	Of great interest	Interested sometimes	Of no interest
Listening to people's problems			
Providing advice			
Ordering, processing and retrieving data, facts and figures			
Writing policies and procedures			
Negotiating and bargaining			
Growing and caring for living things			
Environmental issues			
Strong scientific or technical orientation			

Are you Happy

Change and evolution of processes			
Public speaking			
Logistics			
List other interests if applicable:			

Skills: Please select an option for each of the following:

Skills	Skills I'm Good At	Skills I would like to learn or improve	Skills I have no interest in developing
Mentoring			
Counselling and advising			
Guiding group discussions/facilitating groups			
Diagnosing and treating			
Representing others			
Acting as a liaison			
Evaluating and screening people			
Persuading – convincing and influencing			
Managing conflict / troubleshooting			
Administration			
Helping or caring for others			
Interviewing and recruiting			
Scheduling and monitoring			

Finding the CEO in You

Skills	Skills I'm Good At	Skills I would like to learn or improve	Skills I have no interest in developing
Teaching and training / Developing others			
Supervising others			
Active listening			
Negotiating and mediating			
Coaching			
Collaborating			
Analysing data – comparing and contrasting			
Researching			
Classifying data and information			
Taking inventory			
Managing money and budgeting			
Accounting – calculating and computing			
Forecasting and estimating			
Record keeping			
Website design			

Skills	Skills I'm Good At	Skills I would like to learn or improve	Skills I have no interest in developing
Programming and computing			
Written communication			
Verbal communication			
Organizing and planning			
Decisive – makes rational and sound decisions			

Are you Happy

Understanding and utilizing social media			
Meeting deadlines – time management skills			
Adaptable to change at work			
Self- management / Disciplined			
Leadership			
Relationship building			
Public speaking and presentation skills			
Flexibility / Adaptable			
Reliability – dependable and trustworthy			
Intuitiveness – perceptive, sensitive and instinctive			
Innovative – creating new processes			
Proactive and self-starting / shows initiative			
Delegating			
Problem solving			
Drive and enthusiasm			
Auditing			
Computer skills			
Influence and negotiation skills			
Strategic planning			
Organizational awareness/ business acumen			
Policy skills–interprets, applies and prepares policies			
Project Management			

Finding the CEO in You

Change Management			
Resilience – perseverance, calm under pressure			
Editing and proofreading			
Utilizing instruments or complex equipment			
Chairing and coordinating meetings			
Critical thinking			
Quality control analysis			
Systems evaluation			
Fair minded and tolerant			
Providing feedback			
Conceptual and analytical ability – dealing with concepts and complexities			
Risk taker			
Team player			
Detail focus – observes fine details and logical sequence			
Integrity – committed, trustworthy and fair			
Rational and logical			
Add additional skills below if needed -			

Values: Please select an option for each of the following values:

Values	Always value	Sometimes value	Seldom Value	Never value

Are you Happy

Advancement – Opportunities for growth and promotion				
Challenging work – to be stretched and intellectually stimulated				
Expertise – demonstrate a high degree of proficiency in job skills				
Work/life balance – juggle personal interests and demands with work				
Independence – to be autonomous and work without direction				
Recognition – receive credit for good work				
Flexibility – flexible work schedule				
Belonging/Affiliation – feel a sense of belonging				
Change and variety – different experiences, responsibilities and activities				
Help others – contributing to helping people directly				
Calm atmosphere – minimal pressure and avoid the 'rat race'				
Leadership –being in charge, leading others, prime decision maker				
Work alone – work independently with minimal contact from others				
Decision making – making choices about what to do and how to do it				
Creativity – conceive new ideas and programs, think outside the box.				
High earnings – money, wealth				
Status and prestige – impress or gain respect by level of my job				
Structured environment – work routine and duties are largely predictable and not likely to change				
Teamwork – work with others towards a common goal				

Finding the CEO in You

Personal growth- grow as a person and learn new ideas and sills				
Cutting edge – work at the frontier of knowledge				
Community – to help assist society and touch the community				
Spirituality				
Competitiveness – internal and external competition, to perform better than others				
Authority – in control of my work and the positions of others				
Collaboration – assistance and support within the team				
Integrity – trust and respect in the workplace				
Security- feel secure at work				
Order – work in an organised and tidy environment with streamlined processes				
Loyalty – dedication and commitment				
Aesthetics – work in a an environment that is physically pleasing				
Adventure – excitement at work with possible risks				
Health and wellbeing				
Social – belong to a social environment, with regular contact with people				
Environmental consciousness				
Competence – do work properly				
Add additional values below if needed –				

Are you Happy

Now that you know what you're good at, you've taken the first step toward finding the expertise in you. You're ready for the next question?

What do you enjoy doing? The list for this can be endless as well. There are so many things to choose from. There is NO wrong answer here. Just write down what you enjoy doing. Do you like making thing? Do you like to paint, draw, or take pictures? What types of recreational activities do you like doing? Is reading a passion of yours, or do you like daring activities like snowboarding? Do you like spending time with children or elderly people? Is cooking your thing? Do you like to play? Yes, you read right…play! Some people don't, if you do, write it down. Now what do you like to play: board games like chess, video games, or maybe group games such as charades? Put them on the list of things you enjoy. This should be easy for you if you don't think too much about. Everyone knows what they like to do, so start writing.

What excites you? The word "excite" means different things to different people. Whatever it means to you, write down what excites you. What excites you may not excite everyone. That's fine. It's not supposed to. You are your own, individual person. You can ask two different people, and you'll probably get two different answers, because different things excite different people. If you're the snowboarding, bungee jumping kind of person, you'll want a career that keeps your adrenaline flowing. You may be a total opposite. You may get excited about working with numbers and enjoy being an accountant. Which one is right? Both of them. It's about you and what excites you.

You can actually take things you enjoy and things that excite you and turn them into a career choice you'll be excited about doing. Doesn't that sound awesome? I know it does, so start writing that list of things that excite you. I don't care if it's trying various flavors of bubble gum, write it down. You never know which thing that excites you will be able to be an excellent career for you.

What is something you know that most others don't know? You're first reaction to this may be nothing, but I bet you're wrong. The key word here is "most" others. Do you know or understand something that your family and/or friends don't know how to do? It doesn't have to be something major. Make a list of things. Can you do speak French? Can you crochet? Do you know how to make others laugh? Do you know a few secret family recipes? You may be surprised at the people who would love to have that knowledge, so think of everything you can.

What is something you'd do even if you didn't get paid for it? This is probably easy for you. Start by looking at things you already do that you don't get paid for. What parts of your current job do you take on as extra assignments that you don't get paid extra to do? What are some things you from the list of things you enjoy doing that you're going to continue to do if you never get paid for them?

See how it works. All of these things work together and lead to the job you'll love doing and one you can be paid well for.
Maybe if you like cooking, you're good at it, and passionate about it, you could blog about recipes or do videos creating meals. It's about taking who you are and capitalizing on the strengths you have.
Forget your weaknesses. Focus on the best you have to give and the things you most enjoy. Maybe you love numbers. You're good at math, but standing in front of a classroom would freak you out.
That doesn't mean you can't start a blog where readers can write in problems and you can help them solve them or you couldn't do a short video about some type of problem.

From this point on…Think Positive! As you begin to see the many career options online, think of all the work you've just done. Look at the lists and see how you could various parts of what you are good at and love doing to make money from home. It might just be something you want for a little extra, but it can be much more if you're dedicated to it. You have the power within you to reach your maximum potential and monetize the expertise you have.

Remember…only positive thoughts. Don't think about what you can't do or could never do…think only about what you CAN do. Don't think about what you hate…think only about what you LOVE. Remember, it' the combination that you're looking for.

Are you Happy

How to Monetize on Your Expertise

There are people that make money every day using their expertise online. Think you couldn't do it…think again! These are ordinary people who finally learned to stop focusing on their negative aspects and focus on what they CAN do. They know what they're good at and enjoy doing and they put it to work for them so they can monetize their expertise.

Here are a few ways you can do it:

START A BLOG—If you don't like to write, this may not be a good option for you. Blogging is either inexpensive or free, depending on where you blog. Blogging can be done for various reasons. People often use blogs to promote themselves and the work they do, and it is a good means of social media marketing. Blogging can, however, become a full-time job. There is a lot of work to do to keep up with your blog, but you can make money. It won't happen overnight, however, so don't quit your day job.

Blogging is a way for you to work telling about something you're passionate about and enjoy doing. You can enrich the lives of other through your blog. It may take a while to build a community, but it will happen over time if you work at it.

Ways to make money blogging

There's more than one way for a blogger to make money. The two major ways are through affiliate marketing and ads. Here's how they work:

Ads

The first goal you have to reach to make money with your blog is to get your blog to where it's popular.

Once it is, you can sell advertising space on your blog. You simply find advertisers and they pay you a few either monthly, weekly, or quarterly. You need to get as much traffic to your site as possible. Sometimes,

bloggers use networks such as Google Adsense. They'll help by matching ads with blogs that are relevant

Affiliate Marketing

This is a good choice, because it's easier. You become an affiliate with a company/product such as GoDaddy.com, for example. On your blog, you promote the companies/products you are affiliated to and use links in your blog that will direct your audience to their company. When someone clicks on the link you have in your blog, you automatically get a percentage of any sales made from that sale.

Don't mislead your readers! Actually try what you promote. If you send your reader to something that won't value them in anyway or worse, is a bad company/product, you could lose the reader. Adding benefit, however, will not only keep them reading, it will keep them clicking. They'll also pass on the link for your blog to their friends.

Choosing what to promote
If this sounds good to you, then you're probably wondering what types of products you can promote. What you sell will depend greatly on what type of blog you write, obviously. For example: You wouldn't market dog food on a dating tip blog. You want to market things that are related to what you're writing about and relevant to the people who read them.

One easy way is to promote yourself and merchandise you can sell. If you like to write, you can do eBooks, which we'll discuss later, and sell them on your site.
You may want to teach them something and do an ecourse. At first you might find that difficult, but you'll be surprised at how easily you can pick that up.

You may want to have products available to sell on your site. If you have the right type of blog, you might be able to have products made such as: coffee mugs, t-shirts, mouse pads, water bottles, etc and sell them on your blog.

Are you Happy

Income amount that is possible from a blog

I can't give you an exact dollar amount you'll make from blogging, but I can tell you how much you'll make from not blogging—Zero!

There are a lot of factors that affect how much money your blogs make. Thing like:

The traffic you're able to draw to your site

What the content of your blog is

How much and what kind of marketing you do for the blog

How dedicated you are to it and what your work ethic is.

Your niche and the value you are giving your reader

The truth is, you might have a good blog, and still not make money. It really does depend on the above-
mentioned things. You'll never know if you don't try, so if you think writing a blog is for you…go for it!

Getting started in blogging

Once you have decided on the concept, you can get it started quickly. In just a few minutes you can go to sites like WordPress or Blogger and create the blog.
Then you just need to get it launched and promote it.

Concept development

You've already figured out what you're good at and enjoy. You've followed the guidelines and see where these cross over and determined how you can take those things and actually make money from them.

Finding the CEO in You

This is going to be something you are no doubt passionate about. You're going to have to keep new content on your blog to keep your readers coming back. Here are a few things you can do

Share a unique point of view about the topic that you feel that needs to be shared.

If food is your passion, share what you cook with your audience. You can do this by writing recipes. You might want to go to various restaurants and then share how you thought the food was. People are interested in these types of reviews, especially from new restaurants they want to try. No one likes a bad meal!

If you enjoy going to movies, you could always go and then write a review for it. People like movies of all kinds. If you do it right and add things they can't find anywhere else, your blog will probably do well.

Most men and a few women I know are really into cars. If automobiles are your thing, there are several things you can do. Put pictures of model you like on your blog. Attend car shows and write about all the different models that were there. If you're more into the mechanics of cars, you can do a simple blog on "how to" fix small things that are wrong with your car yourself. If you save a reader money, you can be guaranteed they'll be back.

Ways to benefit your reader.

Trying to write a blog on a lot of topics usually doesn't work. Find your niche in the world and stick to it. This will give your blog purpose, and helps the reader know you mean business. You're there to help your viewers and they'll know it. They'll begin to feel that you really have expertise in your chosen area and they will begin to trust you.

There are many different ways you can help people. Here are a few:

- Tell them "how to" do something—If there's something you are excited about, have experience in, and know well, you can share that knowledge with your readers.

Are you Happy

- Keep them updated on what's going on—If there's a new development that you feel is related to your topic and your readers would like to know, you can share it with them. .
- Inspiration from life experiences—Life sometimes throws us for a loop. Challenging and difficult experiences happen every day. Think about your life. Have you had an experience like this that you were able to overcome? You can
- These are just a few, but they're major ones. As you can see, you probably are able to share something with the world.
- Pick a catchy name—You want something that will stand out, but still give the reader a hint about what your blog is about. Just brainstorm or ask family and friends what they think would be good. .

Know about keywords—Keywords are the big thing these days. They're words that will help you show up in searches and help readers find you. If you go to Google Adwords, they have a keyword tool that will help you. It's easy to use, and you'll get a great benefit from it. You want a much traffic as possible, and keywords help you get it.

You can search by individual words, phrases, or websites for keywords. Just type in things that are related to your topic. Sometimes you can use your keywords when you write. As long as you use them effectively.

Pick a site to host your blog. For the purpose of this book, I'll just explain one.   Blogger.com is a site owned by Google. The way it is designed, you can set up your blog and maintain it regularly in a hassle-free, easy way. Since Google owns it, you'll have the power of Google search behind you to help with traffic.
They offer two options:

Custom domain name—This will cost you about $10 per year

BlogSpot domain name—This option is free of charge

Setting up a Blogger.com Blog

Finding the CEO in You

Go to Blogger—When you get there you can log into your Google account. If you don't have one, they're easy to sign up for with a few easy steps.

Look for the New Blog button—Once you've found it, simply click on it.

Blog name and address—You'll find a place to type in the name you want for your blog and the address you want. Simply type it in.

Templates—The template is how you want it to be set up and what you want it to look like. It gives you several options to choose from. You simply select the one you want. If you'd rather create the template later, you can do that too.

Blog—It's time to begin blogging. You'll find a button that says "Create Blog." Click on it to begin.

Name it—After you type in your text, name the blog post. Then just find "Publish" and click.

Getting your blog "out there"

A great blog does no good if it isn't read. You need to promote your blog as much as you can. If you don't have any social media accounts, like Twitter or Facebook for example, you need to start at least one. Share your blog with all your friends. They'll share with friends who will share with friends…you get the picture. It's great promotion for your blog and will help you get started.

Blogger has an "About Me" section. First, you'll want to list your blog and then tell potential readers a bit about you so they'll see the skills you have and decide whether or not they want to read your blog. Let them know how you know what you're talking about as well a background info.

You'll want to build a good rapport with other bloggers. If they click "Like" for your blog, then give them the courtesy of visiting their site as well. You can write a comment or return the "Like." another blogger "Likes" your site, then go to his or her site and either "Like" if you like it.

The best way to get traffic to your blog is good content. This doesn't just mean quality up-to-date information, although that is imperative for success.   Make sure you've used the proper grammar and punctuation. You want to look like a professional if you expect others to think you are.

POST A VIDEO—All around the world there are people of all ages uploading videos online. A great number of these have viewers anxiously waiting for the next one. How do they do it?

Maybe you don't like to write, but don't have a problem talking about the things you love. Instead of writing a blog, you can do simple video of the information you want to share. Before you brush this option off as silly, you should know that posting a video on YouTube can be profitable for you. You can even write a blog and do a video. That way those who like to read and don't like to view videos get the info as well as those who don't like to read getting the convenience of watching the video. Think—Double Profits!

Making money with Videos
There's a program for video makers can to earn money from advertising. It's called the Partner Program. If you're a regular video up-loader, and you have a good sized number of viewers, this could be for you. Through this program you share in the profit they get from people who watch your video. If you're in the Partner Program, you have to allow YouTube to put ads that are relevant beside your posts.

You can also make money on this program by allowing advertisements in your videos. These can be annoying, but they can also make you money. If they place an ad in your video, an advertiser will pay more for it than just one beside your video.

As long as you regularly upload videos that are original to YouTube, you can apply to be a partner. Of course, you also need to have your video viewed by thousands of people. If you want to use anything with visual or audio clips, the proper agreements must be made with regard to copyrights.

Like blogging, there's no way you can really determine how much money you'll make. It's a shot in the dark, but hey…at least it's a shot! You'll be doing something you like to do anyway, so why not try to make money from it. Who knows? Your video just might be the next one to go viral and make you a lot of money.

Read the fine print

Before you begin uploading videos, make sure you read the fine print and know what you're getting into. It says you still retain the copyright, but you're granting "limited" rights.

These are granted not only to YouTube, but also to the millions of people who use YouTube.

Write an eBook—We live in a technical world. It's hard to find anything that isn't available electronically. A lot of people prefer to get their information digitally. They always have the newest device in their hands, and a lot of them read eBooks. In case you've been living under a rock for the past few years, the word "eBook" stands for electronic book.
Even though you may have known what it was, you might not have known that you can write and publish an eBook and make money from it.

Making money from an ebook

One of the great things about eBook writing and publishing is that you can do it all yourself. If you select the right topic and choose and market to the right target market, you can publish an eBook on just about anything. There are people out there who want to know what you know. They want to know how to do it, and they're willing to pay for it. It's a simple process that can turn your passion into profit.

Another great thing about an eBook is that they don't have to be novels. They're much shorter than your average book, so they're easier to write. Let's say you take your passion and write a nice little "how to" eBook. If it becomes an eBook that is in demand, you can make pretty good money. Let's say you write an eBook on "Disciplinary skills to tame the wild child." It might only be 25-50 pages, so let's just figure on selling it for $20. If you market it right, and use the right keywords to increase traffic to your site, people will probably want to buy it. For the purposes of this book, let's just take the low end and say you make one sale a day. That's $140 a week = $560 a month = $6,720 a year. That may not sound like a lot. When you consider, however, the hours it took you to write it, that's very good money. Even if it took you 10 hours to write, which it probably wouldn't if you got down to business, you would be making $672 an hour. Do you make that much on your day job? Even if it took you 100 hours to write it, you'd still be making $67.20 an hour.

That's good money.

There's no way to determine exactly how much you'll make. It could be more, or it could be less, but you'll never know if you don't try. Write one, promote it, and give it a shot. If it doesn't work, try it again. The important thing is that you're actually doing something to monetize your skills.

Just think if you started a blog on the topic, uploaded videos on the same topic, and sold your book from both your blog and using links from your video. That's triple the money from one thing you do well.

Have I piqued your interest? If so, let me tell you how you go about writing eBooks and making money online. It's easier than you might think.

Choose your market—If you have several things you're good at and you enjoy, do research to see what's selling online. Make a list of everything you can think of you could write about. Decide which niche you feel confident about has the most buyers and go with it.

Develop an outline—Behind every good book, there is a good outline. You want your eBook to be organized and easy to read. Writing an outline helps you organize your thoughts, and will also make it easier to write. You can play around with chapters, and move things from one place to another until you feel you've got it right. It's a lot easier than moving it after you've written it.

Write the book—Begin writing your eBook. If you follow your outline, you'll be surprised at how easy it can be. It may take you a few books to really get the hang of it, but don't give up.

Edit the book—Even the best of writers won't get it perfectly on the first shot. You want to make sure you edit your book. Read it carefully to make sure what you wrote will make sense to someone else. Also correct all of your punctuation and grammar errors. With spell check, there's no excuse for these types of errors.

Get it ready—Get the digital product compiled and ready for sale.

Sales letter—Your potential buyers will want to know what the book is about and how it will benefit them. In other words, if it doesn't benefit them, they probably won't buy it. Explain all of that in a sales letter.

Domain name—Select a good domain name. Make sure it is available, and register it.

Web hosting service—You'll need to find a good web hosting service. You'll want one that is dependable, because you're going to use it to sell your eBook.

Create a website—You'll want to have a site or blog. When you post on your social media sites, you can give links to your site or blog.

"Buy Now" button—There are several dependable electronic payment systems online. Once you choose the types of payment, you'll want to add a "Buy Now" button for the convenience of the buyer. This is a lot easier, for you as well. You'll want to select one that has reasonable fees for the transactions.

Are you Happy

Market your eBook—The greatest of books won't sell if no one knows about it. It is up to you to promote and advertise your book if you want to make money. Social media marketing is a great place to start. If you've never had a marketing class, and feel like you couldn't sell water in the desert, there are many sites available online to help you. Don't just go with one source. Check out several. If you find the same advice on them, then it's probably good advice.

You may never write a best-selling eBook, but that doesn't mean you can't till make money. If your goal is to make it your source of income, it will take time and practice. Just remember the old saying, "If at first you don't succeed, try, try again

Coach/Mentor others—Do you enjoy helping others? If so, this may be the way you can make money online. Maybe you've retired and feel bored with nothing to occupy the time you used to spend working. If you were really good at what you did, and feel you could help others, maybe you should consider being a coach or mentor.

You can make money doing this, but it depends on your training and experience as well as how well you market yourself as a coach/mentor. For small mentoring jobs that will only take a session or two, an hourly fee is usually used. For continued mentoring, a monthly or weekly rate may apply.

What you need to do

If you think this might be something you'd be good at and want to give it a try, there are a few things you need to do:

Profile—The first thing you need to do is create yourself a profile. Tell everyone about who you are and how you can help them. Include all the experience and expertise you have. You'll also want to tell things you're interested in to give them a more complete picture.

Time Limits—How much time do you want to commit to mentoring each week? Don't jump in over your head. It may be best to commit to small amount of time and increase as you learn what is involved and the work necessary. Whatever program you choose once you commit, you are agreeing to the time requirement they require.

Find a good program—If you don't have a clue how to go about that, you might want to try doing a search for online mentoring. If you find the right site, you'll find a list of all the opportunities that are available. They should also be able to tell you what is mentoring in that field involves.

Ask questions—Sometimes you can thoroughly read the description of what a company thinks mentoring involves, but you're still not sure. For example, you might have mentoring once a week in mind, and they might want two to three times a week. If it's not clear, ask. Also clarify any other questions.

Wait for approved profile—There is a mentor profile form online that you need to fill out. You can't just fill it out and become a mentor. You need to wait for approval from that organization.

The organization will let you know when they have someone they feel is a match for you. They'll give you instructions to follow and you can be on your way to a career as a mentor. You'll also be on your way to helping someone else be successful in life. That should make you feel good about yourself.

If you feel like you have a wealth of information, but just don't know how to share it, you can find many training courses that will teach you how to be a mentor. That way, you can become a certified mentor/coach, which may add to your ability to sell your services.

These courses are easy to sign up for, and usually include practice coaching sessions you need to complete before certification. If so, your client will have to send verification that you did the hours. At the end of the courses, you'll be tested before you receive certification.

Are you Happy

If you have a degree in business, there is always a market for business coaches. Maybe you created a successful business from the ground up. Someone just starting a business could greatly benefit from what you have to offer. They could learn from your experiences and from your mistakes. Sometimes, we learn more from mistakes than successes.

If you have a degree, you don't need certification through a coaching program, but you may want to take one a course if you're not sure you could pass your information on to someone else effectively. One of the key skill a business coach must have is the ability to be a good listener. They'll also be able to think and plan a program of development for the person they're mentoring.

There are many areas of business, so you'll want to find the niche that best suits you. What is it you're best at and enjoy the most in the field? You'll be able to effectively pass on things you're passionate about.

You can join a coaching firm, or set up a business on your own. Established firm, however, are a good entry point and will help you gain experience in the field of mentoring. If you decide to go the self-employed route and set up your own business, remember that marketing is the key. No one will hire you for their mentor/coach if they've never heard of you.

Everything we've mentioned this far can be applied to your career choice of being a mentor/coach. You can create a website, have a blog, post videos, and write eBooks. One way to get yourself out there is to hold several small business seminars for free. You can use the connections you make to build your reputation. You can also interest people in reading your blogs, watching your video tips, and buying your eBooks that way.

Do a podcast—This I yet another money-making plan to monetize your talents. It is a form of digital media. For a podcast, you record and people subscribe to your audio or video. They are downloaded or streamed online. It can be to either a computer or a mobile device of some kind.   You can develop podcasts that are one download or a series.

Some people do podcasts simply because they're passionate about something and want to share it. While it's OK to start out like this, there's no reason to give your valuable information away for free when people are willing to pay for it. If your following is big enough, you can make a whole career of podcasting.

No podcaster uses the same exact formula for success. What works for one might not work for another. You have to find what works for you. Like mentoring, being a podcaster has a wide-range of payment options. It depends on your niche, your knowledge, your experience, how well you market it, and how big the demand is for what you're podcasting.

Here are a few helpful tips to help you if you feel like you'd like to give it a try:

Build your audience—Building your audience is the only way to be sure you'll make profits in podcasting. There are podcasting networks such as Wizzard Media, Podtrac, and Mevio that love to have podcasters with big audiences.

Find sponsors—If you'd like, you can try to find sponsors for yourself. You may be able to do it, but be sure you realize the workload involved.

Seek donations—It works for public TV, so why not for podcasting. Sometimes you have to do things to get yourself out there. If you can't find sponsors and want to build your audience, you can set up a button on your site that informs the prospective audience that the show will available to them for a donation. You won't make a lot of money this way, but you will get people to see what you have to offer. After your audience builds, you can charge a fee.

Go 50/50—Give away some things and charge for others. If they buy something, they get something else for free. It usually doesn't even have to be much. It's just the principal of getting something free that will make the sale. After all, if you're selling something that is the same price and quality as another persons and you offer something free, it makes good sense that they'd go with the person who was also giving them something free. Everyone likes to feel they are not only getting their money's worth—they want to get more for their money.

Show them a little of your information—This means let them see a little bit of what you have to offer. Make it good enough that they will want to see more. Don't make the free stuff junk. Give them a really good solid piece of information, or let them know how you can benefit them, but they'll need to buy it all to get those benefits. Usually when you do these, they run about 20 minutes of good information. Don't forget…how you benefit them is important. If you make this information valuable, and they see how it will work for them, they'll want more. If you have a series of podcasts, they'll want them all.

Create your own network—This definitely isn't going to be something that comes overnight. Building a podcast network, however, is far simpler than building a radio or television network. Once you're able to set one up, you can lineup your programming, and sell advertising for all the different categories you have. This will make you a lot of money.

Create a brand—Being completely unknown can make it difficult to get started making money from podcasting. Often, having a catchy brand name for yourself and your information can increase your income to triple what you got before. Sometimes, it can increase even more.

iPhone app—You can also sell these apps along with your podcast. Sometimes, you can offer your service for free and make money from a simple iPhone app that only costs the viewer $3.99. You can do this through a program by Wizzard Media. You simply agree to share the revenue.
When you think of the millions of iPhone users, this is something worth looking into.

Sponsorship + editorials—You can take your show's editorials and combine them with sponsorship. If you find companies that have products or services that are also used digitally, they'll be more likely to sponsor your podcast.

Digital audio book seller is one of these that often does this. It works easily if you recommend their books, which some of your viewers probably read anyway.

It doesn't matter which form of online money making you choose. You can choose one or even all of the above. The goal is to just focus on giving your audience great advice and tips they can really put to use. If you do that and market it correctly, you can achieve your goal of making money online and you can do it using something you enjoy doing.

Just think how great that would be. Wouldn't you just love to not have to get out of bed early everyday and trudge off to work? You shouldn't run out and quit your day job yet, because it does take time, but it can happen if you want it badly enough.

You've looked at what you do well, what you like, what you're passionate about, what you enjoy, and what you'd do for free. Use that information and take the time to search yourself.

Find something that crosses over in those categories. Think about how you can take that and put it to work for you online.

If you need help figuring it out, ask for the opinion of others you trust, and determine what that something is. Once you figure it out, the hard part is over. Think about it carefully. You've got skills and knowledge others will pay to know. How can you take what you're good at and passionate about and best share your skills and knowledge with other people who need to know that same information?

Once you've done that, select the method of online money making that you feel best suits you. You may start as a once-a-week blogger, and love it so much you do it daily and your readers grow the more you blog.

Are you Happy

You may then decide a video would be great too so you could expand your audience. Hey, while you're on a roll, why not write an eBook. Even if you give it away, you'll still increase traffic on your blog. I think you understand what I'm trying to get across to you. It's simple. You have the roadmap—you just need to take the first step. From there, where you'll travel can be an endless journey of success.

Nike's slogan is important to remember when you're thinking about putting your expertise to work for you online.

You've determined what you're good at and what you love to do. You have to make the choice of whether or not to combine these things and begin to use them in an enjoyable, profitable way.

Stop complaining about the job you do and start loving the job you do. It doesn't matter how good you are at what you're doing now if you're unhappy.

There's no reason to go through life not living up to your full potential. You want to make money online, or you wouldn't have read this book.

That indicates that either you're not happy with what you're doing or you need to make extra money by working at home. Whatever the reason is, you've wasted the time it took you to read if you don't apply anything you've learned.

Getting started making money online is not as difficult as you imagined it was. You know that now. You know what to do. It's time to be like Nike, and "Just DO it!"

Finding the CEO in You

~Thoughts~

Are You Happy

Part IV

Pursue You Passion

Are You Happy

Chapter 27
Find Your Passion

    Everyone has a passion. It often manifests during childhood and is pursued through play or it is stumbled upon as we age but almost immediate put aside for more practical things like work and building a family. Children are free to actively pursue the things that interest them, but as they age they are encouraged to go after more practical pursuits often putting their passion aside. However, it isn't impossible or impractical to continue to follow your passion even as you age. Doing what you love even as a hobby can go a long way to living a life that you enjoy. There was a time when people weren't encouraged to follow or even consider passion when living their lives. Survival was the most important and that often meant working from sun up to sundown with only room for sleeping and eating. Things like hobbies and passion weren't discussed or even considered because there was no room for it.

Are You Happy

Thanks to societal changes like the Industrial Revolution and the advent of technology, we no longer have to toil so hard just to survive. We have the luxury of only having to work 40 hours a week (give or take) and having weekends off to do things like goof off, go on vacation or discover and pursue our passion. With our overly scheduled lives that might not seem like much time but any time spent actively seeking your heart's desire is better than no time at all. Over time, we often forget the passions of our childhood or even the ones we discover as we age. So discovering our passion is often the first step down a path of actively pursuing it. If you're unsure how to go about discovering your passion, here are some steps to get you thinking in the right direction.

1.Take a stroll down memory lane and make a list.

Think back to when you were a kid. What are some of the things you really loved doing? What are some of the things you thought were really cool but couldn't do? What are some of the things you really wanted to try but didn't think you'd be good at it? Write everything down, no matter how silly it may sound. This is a great time to throw practicality completely out of the window and live in a fantasy land, even if only for a moment. Take some time with this but not too long. You don't want to spend the rest of your days dreaming about what your passion could be. You want to actually pursue it!

_____

_____

_____

_____

_____

_____

_____

2. Consider your current job. What are some things that you are tasked with doing at work that you enjoy?

While this may not be as fun as strolling down memory lane, it's important to consider what you enjoy doing as an adult. Make a separate list. It may be best to do this while you're actually at work so you can fully assess your daily tasks. Write down everything that comes to mind even the most mundane tasks. While it may not seem very cool to write that you enjoy creating spreadsheets or collating papers, it still counts. Passion isn't always considered cool or trendy but if you love it, you should explore it.

3. What would you do if you had all of the money you needed and didn't have to worry about paying your bills?

Are You Happy

We all have to work to live. Yes we no longer have to work from sun up to sun down just to put food on the table (for the most part), but we still have bills to pay and mouths to feed (even if it's just your own mouth). This is another fun exercise and you're allowed to be as fanciful as you like. Practicality has no place in the world where all of our financial responsibilities are met and we're able to just live as we please. Make a separate list.

Now that you have these three lists, review them. You may notice some similarities between the lists. Take note of the similarities. If you're a fan of color coding, you can color code them or you can just make a separate list. The similarities you discover will lead you down the road to pursuing your passion. In fact, you may find some passions that are ripe for you to begin exploring right away. However, don't throw away the other lists. Keep them in a safe place that you can easily access. Some of the other things on your list may be worth exploring at a later date. Even if it's an interest on one list, it could still take you down a path to your passion. The cool thing about passions is that they can often lead to other things you really enjoy.

The next step in this process is to go out and do some of the things from your final list. Approach this process in an exploratory manner, don't rush it. Finding your passion shouldn't be approached like a timed task. The whole point is to discover things that you enjoy and then do them. I realize that may be easier said than done but it's an important step in the process. So now that you have a list of some things you'd like to explore, you may be unsure how to proceed. Here are some tips on how to dig further into your newfound passion journey.

1.Take a class

There are tons of classes, both online and offline on almost any topic around. Do a quick web search for your topic and "class" to see what types of classes are available. For example, if one thing you wanted to do as a kid was climb trees and you live in Boston, do a web search of "climb trees class" or "climb trees class Boston" and you will begin to find classes, courses and articles about climbing trees and the ones specific to the Boston area.

2.Join a group

There is a wonderful website called www.meetup.com where people are encouraged to create groups around a specific interest. I encourage everyone to create a profile on meetup.com. It's free to join and is a great resource. Once you create a profile, you can do a search for any interest and the site will show you all of the groups related to that interest in your area. Then you can join the groups and participate in their meetups. The different groups are free to join for the most part. The ones that require a fee are typically very affordable and may be worth the extra investment. It's a great way to not only explore your interests but meet other people who share your interests and possibly make new friends.

3.Read a book

If you're not feeling particularly adventurous at the moment but still want to dive into these interests you forgot you had, reading is a great way to explore it without leaving your house. While I do encourage you to eventually get out into the world and actually explore your interests through action, reading is a good step. You

Are You Happy

can do a search of your favorite online book seller, visit your local bookstore or spend some time in your local library. Get as many books as you can read at one time and spend some time between those pages exploring your interests.

Chapter 28
Find Your Passion's Skill Set

Congratulations! You've started down the path of finding your passion. By now you should have at least identified a few things that you are passionate about and be exploring at least one or two of them. Hopefully, you're enjoying this foray into fun and learning more about yourself. In the meantime, let's get back to why you stopped pursuing your passions in the first place; practicality.

Many of the things we're passionate about aren't really the most practical things to do when you grow up and become a "responsible" adult (Let's be honest. Who actually feels like a responsible adult when you become one?). Once you've settled into "real life" and started working and taking care of all of the not so fun adult responsibilities, you may find it challenging to do things that don't contribute to your personal bottom line. It may feel indulgent to take time off to do things like fly kites or write short stories when they don't directly contribute to maintaining your household. So while you may do them occasionally, they will often be put off when more pressing "responsible" concerns arise like having to take the car in for repairs or take the kids to their extracurricular activities.

While doing something purely for enjoyment may feel indulgent, most passion pursuits require a level of skill. Some people really enjoy building websites and that's obviously a marketable skill but if your passion is more obscure, it may be tough to find the practical skills behind it. Don't give up and move on to something that you kind of like and abandon your passion, though. It is possible to find the practical skills behind your passion. I'm going to take two examples of passions, one more common and the other more fanciful and show you how it can be done.

Writing Short Stories

Let' start with the more common one. There are many secret writers out there who love to create poetry or prose be it non-fiction or fiction but we all know that most authors don't end up on the best seller list. In fact, most writers never make a dime from their writings. But just because they may not profit from their narrative musings, it doesn't mean that writers aren't building a skill set. While it may seem obvious, there are some skills there that might not be so immediately noticeable as well as the more obvious ones. There are some steps to discover these skills.

1. Take an objective look at what you do as a writer.

When you sit down to write something, take a moment and jot down all of the things that you're doing or are about to do. For example:

   a. Create a story
   b. Organize the idea
   c. Create characters
   d. Research/describe the setting of the story
   e. Commit to a project from start to finish

2. Research the job descriptions of writers. Do a web search for "writer job description". This will give you some great insight into the skills built through writing.

   a. Make a list of the skills you find in a few of the job descriptions.
   b. Go through the list and pull out skills that you feel apply best to you and add them to the first list.

3. Research writers' websites and look at the services they provide. These services might give you some insight into skills you hadn't considered. Add them to your list.

4. Go to writing events and talk to other writers. There are conferences, festivals and networking events for a wide variety of topics. Find local writing events by doing a web search. Not only will you learn about the skills that you have developed, you might meet some cool new writing friends to support you in following your passion.

Flying Kites

Are You Happy

Now we can move to a more fanciful hobby like flying kites. It may be tough to see that there are practical skills involved in this particular hobby but there are. For this example, we're going to assume that you also enjoy creating and building kites. Let's go through the same steps.

1. Take an objective look at what you do as a kite flyer.

   a. Visualize the kite
   b. Draw the vision
   c. Figure out the materials you plan to use
   d. Map out how you plan to put it together
   e. Build the kite
   f. Test the kite
   g. Tweak the kite in case it doesn't fly properly the first time
   h. Commit to a project from start to finish

2. Research job descriptions of kite flyers and builders. You may not think these descriptions exist but you'd be surprised at the types of jobs that exist. Kite flying might very well be a viable job somewhere so it doesn't hurt to look.

3. Do some video website research. Find a how to video on kite making and make note of the steps. Then go through the steps objectively and pull out any skills you notice.

4. Research festivals, events and conferences related to kite building. Many of the more obscure or fanciful passions have festivals, events and parties created around them. These events will often have seminars and workshops that discuss the more technical aspects of

the hobby. This is a great place to find those hidden skills you may be developing by building and flying kites. As an added bonus, you will begin to meet people who share your passion and might make some new friends.

As you can see, it is very possible to find practical skills that are being developed by pursuing your passion. Plus since it's something you truly enjoy doing and actively pursue, you're going to be really good at it.

Chapter 29
Scale Your Passion

Are You Happy

In the entrepreneur community, scale, is a very popular word. It can mean several different things but in this case, it means growth. If you are able to take your passion and turn it into a business, that's a wonderful thing and should be applauded. If you can take that same business and successfully scale it, that should be commended. While it may seem like an unnecessary factor to consider, there are many businesses that make income but can't handle explosive or consistent growth. Some businesses are created to be and remain small. There's absolutely nothing wrong with keeping your work load small and easy to manage but if you want to turn your passion into a viable business that supports and sustains you, it has to be created to grow.

For example, if your passion is writing short stories, you can make money by writing short stories for other people. If it takes you three days to write and edit a complete story and you work on your stories Monday-Friday from 9am-4pm, you would only be able to churn out about 1.5 stories a week. If somehow the word got out and 5 people asked you to write a story a piece and they were all due in one week, you'd end up working a lot of overtime or have to turn away potential clients. This business model is not built to scale. You are limited to the number of stories you can produce and if you want to get more clients, you'd have to adjust your hours, write stories faster or hire other writers. It can be hard to make those kinds of changes once you've started working. But if you go into it knowing that those things will have to happen, you are more apt to be prepared when the time comes. One reason why many new businesses fail in the first three years of existence is that they're not built to properly handle growth. Yes, a lot of customers is a good problem to have but only if you can take advantage of the opportunity.

There are definitely some other processes that can be put in place to help with scalability like automating or outsourcing some of your business tasks. But with any process, it takes time and preparation to really benefit from them. When you are creating a business, it's ultimately up to you as the owner to consider your long term goals and what needs to happen to successfully grow your business. This is best done early on.

Finding the CEO in You

Chapter 30

Live Your Passion with Intention

Once you've identified your passion and found some practical uses for it, the hard part comes next. Living your passion won't be easy. You may find yourself having to defend it to family and friends. While standing up for your passion may be a challenge, it won't be the hardest one. You will have to consistently work with yourself to stay true to doing what you love. If you've made it all the way to adulthood without pursuing your passion, there's sometimes a very compelling reason; fear. It's not easy to put yourself out there to potentially be judged, especially if your passion is considered impractical. It can also be scary to do something that you aren't familiar with or comfortable doing. This fear is natural and shouldn't be used as an excuse not to move forward. If you have found something that you enjoy, it's worth it to pursue it.

Another thing that prevents more people from following their passion is failure. The fear of failure is one of the strongest and most paralyzing ones. However, the fear of success may be just as strong. Sometimes it's easier to simply sit and dream about what could be than it is to actually go out and do it. Both success and failure carry with them their own level of responsibility but in either case, you've made the first step and tried.

"Our deepest fear is not that we are inadequate. Our deepest fear is that we are powerful beyond measure. It is our light, not our darkness that most frightens us. We ask ourselves, 'Who am I to be brilliant, gorgeous, talented, fabulous?' Actually, who are you not to be?
— Marianne Williamson, Return to Love: Reflections on the Principles of "A Course in Miracles"

We can often be our own worst critics, especially when it comes to stepping outside of our own box and doing something different. Negative and doubtful self-talk is natural but it shouldn't stop you. Neither should you not knowing what to do next. Yes, I've given you some steps to follow but if you noticed, many of them involved doing some research. We live in a society where information is an important commodity and it's very readily available Take advantage of it.

    Just as not following your passion brings with it the responsibility of a dream unfulfilled, following your passion and being successful brings with it the responsibility that comes with that success. The great thing about following through with something that's risky is that even if you do fail, you can rest comfortably knowing that you tried. If you do nothing at all, you never know what could have been. Happiness is a decision. If you make the decision that you are going to follow your passion and that it will make you happy, it will.

Addendum

Are You Happy

True Stories

When you begin to actively follow your passion, it could be an isolating experience. Often your family and friends won't be able to come with you on this journey. But there are a lot of other people out in the world who have taken that plunge and done so successfully. Here are three real people who took their passion and ran with it.

Angela Halsted: Passion is puzzling

Angela Halsted is a mother of who lives in Arlington, VA with her husband and two children. While she lives a happy life as a soccer mom and wife, she had an interest in puzzles-crossword puzzles to be more exact. One day she decided that she wanted to look into her interest to see what was out there. She would fill out crossword puzzles on her own and an internet search lead her to the world of crossword tournaments. She was hesitant but curious enough to check it out. She went and was pleasantly surprised at the number of people there. She struck up a conversation with some people and ended up talking about all of the random and obscure facts that everyone knew about. She was hooked. Since then she has become an active participant in the puzzling community event doing some guest puzzle submissions for publications like The New York Times. She also attends puzzle conventions and competitions and writes for different crossword blogs. While she didn't quit her day job or completely change her lifestyle, she found a way to successfully pursue her passion.

Kevin West: Passion is jamming

Kevin West is an editor of a magazine who fell into his passion almost by happenstance. Although he grew up eating strawberry jam and pickled beets canned by his grandmother in his hometown in Eastern Tennessee, he didn't grow up with a passion for doing it himself. It wasn't until he bought an entire flat of strawberries that he found his passion for making jam. After buying the flat, he realized that he would not be able to eat them all before they go bad. Not wanting to waste a good crop of strawberries, he took some of them and made preserves, failing miserably. It was that failure that spurred him to push forward. He knew that preserves should taste a certain way and became determined to replicate the recipe of his grandmother. It took him some time, but he was victorious and created a tasty jar of preserves. Along the way he found his passion in creating jam and preserves. He hasn't quit his day job but canning is a passion that he pursues on a full time basis He shares his passion through his blog and truly lives the canning life. He regularly eats food that he's canned and even encourages novices to take up canning. He is fully immersed in the canning lifestyle.

Jenny Blake: Passion is writing

Jenny was one of the lucky ones. She found a great job that she loved. She made great money working for Google. While she loved her job, something was missing. She had an entrepreneurial spirit and always wanted to strike out on her own but the fear and uncertainty that comes with it kept her from making the leap. Plus her job was great, so she worked to be satisfied with it. She was living the corporate dream with a growing 401k, yearly bonuses and a nice salary. She loved her position and the work that she did at Google but in the mean time she continued to pursue her passion for writing by starting a blog which lead to her writing a book. After much thought, she took a three month leave of absence and self-funded her own book tour. After those three months, she realized that not only could she be an entrepreneur, she could excel at it. She left her job, which was not a popular decision, and is now blogging full time, coaching, speaking and promoting her book project. While she loved her job and all of the comforts it brought, she loves running her own business even more. It wasn't an easy

Are You Happy

decision to walk away from her comfortable life to pursue her passion as a career but she did it and is glad she did.

~Thoughts~

Finding the CEO in You

Part VI
Leadership Strategies

Finding the CEO in You

Are You Happy

Across the years, the perception and definition of leadership have changed. Leadership used to mean a position or a role in a hierarchy. Today, leadership is more of a skill than a role. You can be in a leadership role and have no expertise in leadership.
On the other hand, you can be in a non-leading role but demonstrate a lot of leadership and inspire those around you.

Leadership is one of those skills that never gets old and is always looked up to. Leadership definition can be many things to different people. Start by writing down your definition of leadership.

Leadership, for me, is:

_____
_____
_____
_____
_____
_____
_____
_____
_____
_____

We might have a different definition of leadership than you, but the exercises and techniques that you will learn here will help you become a better leader in your life.

One of the key qualities of leaders is that they are self-starters. That said, you can already check that one of your lists because today, you have chosen to read this book and lead yourself to a self-development adventure!

In this section, we will teach you how to develop your leadership skills, no matter what role you play in your career. The skills you will learn here is a life skill that you can use at work but also in your daily interaction with your family, in your volunteer work or any relationships.

In the next chapters, you will learn about leadership, how it can improve your life, and what techniques or abilities you need to develop to become better at it.

~Thoughts~

CHAPTER 31
EVERYDAY LEADERSHIP AND HOW IT CAN IMPROVE YOUR LIFE

We tend to underestimate our daily actions as an act of leadership. We celebrate significant events, big victories, but not necessarily our small gestures that can change the face of the world. Any daily action has the possibility to change the world of a person who crosses our path. Once you recognize that ability that you have, life becomes a series of opportunities to lead.

Leaders know their goals and do small things every day to reach their goal. But it's not always about them, and they help others to move forward in their projects, to remove their doubts so that they can take action.

In a study comparing average leaders to outstanding leaders, 90% of the variance was due to the Emotional Quotient (EQ). The most crucial factor that will predict if you step up and take the lead in life is your EQ.

Finding the CEO in You

If you compare people in a specific field, it is not their IQ or their personality that will make them successful; it is their EQ. This study also demonstrated that developing leadership skills without considering the cognitive strength of the student-led to minimal improvement in their abilities to lead others. For that reason, we have a whole chapter on self-awareness and personal growth that will help you improve your emotional intelligence.

To be a leader is to be the catalyst of a positive event for others, and thus contribute to their development, help them in a necessary decision-making process. It can seem terrifying when you realize that you have so much impact on others, without knowing it, without being aware of it. It is essential to recognize that we are influential agents, and we have an effect on the lives of others that goes beyond money and power.

When you become a leader in your life, you empower yourself to lead the life of your dream. That is the most beautiful gift you can give yourself, as you will always benefit from the skills, experiences, and knowledge you have acquired on that journey to become a great leader. Some of the benefits are:

- Lead a productive life full of abundance;
- Increase your resilience and ability to perform without feeling the pressure of stress;
- Improve your relationships and how others perceive you;
- Become a better communicator and clearly state your goals;
- Acquire self-awareness, self-confidence, and courage;
- Grow your capacity to be creative and innovative;
- Be perceived as trustworthy and competent by others;
- Be more dependable, reliable, and competent.

In the next chapter, we will explore some facts about leadership and how it impacts our world.

CHAPTER 32
THE TRUTH ABOUT LEADERSHIP

Leadership is not a natural skill in most of us. According to research, the best leaders are the ones that have a growth mindset. A growth mindset is a belief that any skills can be developed with dedication and hard work. That being said, it is a skill that you can develop and acquire with time, patience, and practice.

Leaders have a lot of influences, according to researchers, leaders' behavior can influence the mindset of others, the environment in which they are, the cohesion and efficacy of a group, and it can even influence the amount of conflict that is experienced in the group. Even if only 10% of the population are natural leaders, we will all be asked to demonstrate leadership skills at one point in our life.

The good news is that leadership can be learned, and we hope to help you with this book. The other aspect of great leadership is their ability to be involved and engaged. All the work that you will be doing with this book will allow you to experience, first hand, what it is that you need to develop your leadership skills. Be mindful of that experience, and do not hesitate to use that knowledge and experience in coaching others.

Finding the CEO in You

A study completed with 300,000 business leaders revealed the following top abilities:

- Strategic thinking
- Inspiring and motivating
- Critical thinking, analyzing and problem- solving abilities
- Demonstrating transparency, integrity, and honesty
- Developing others
-
- Driving results
- Communicating in a powerful and effective way
- Building relationships
- Displaying technical or professional expertise
- Creating and innovating

All these skills can be developed and utilized in various areas of your life. In the next chapter, we will explore the following subjects a bit deeper and also provide you with a leadership skill self- assessment.

Leadership Self Assessment

Complete this confidential self-assessment to review your use of the leadership competencies expected of executives. Use the results to create goals for your Executive Development Plan (EDP). Alternatively, you may also ask your manager to rate you, then compare ratings and discuss.

Instructions: Please rate the extent to which you currently demonstrate each of the following, using this scale

1 = low   2 = medium   3 = high

EXECUTIVE CORE QUALIFICATION (ECQ) 1: LEADING CHANGE			
1 = low 2 = medium 3 = high	1	2	3
Creativity and Innovation			
Develops new insights into situations			
Questions conventional approaches			

Are You Happy

Encourages new ideas and innovations			
Designs and implements new or cutting edge programs/processes			
External Awareness			
Understands and keeps up to date on local, national, and international policies and trends that affect the organization and shape stakeholder's views.			
Is aware of the organization's impact on the external environment			
Flexibility			
Is open to change and new information			
Rapidly adapts to new information, changing conditions, or unexpected obstacles			
Resilience			
Deals effectively with pressure			
Remains optimistic and persistent, even under adversity			
Recovers quickly from setbacks			
Strategic Thinking			
Formulates objectives and priorities, and implements plans consistent with long-term interests of the organization in a global environment			
Capitalizes on opportunities and manages risks			

HOW IMPORTANT IS YOUR ABILITY TO LEAD CHANGE?			
EXECUTIVE CORE QUALIFICATION (ECQ) 2: LEADING PEOPLE			
1 = low 2 = medium 3 = high	1	2	3
Conflict Management			
Encourages creative tension and differences of opinions			
Anticipates and takes steps to prevent counterproductive confrontations			

Finding the CEO in You

Manages and resolves conflicts and disagreements in a constructive manner		
Leveraging Diversity		
Fosters an inclusive workplace where diversity and individual differences are valued and leveraged to achieve the vision and mission of the organization		
Developing Others		
Develops the ability of others to perform and contribute to the organization by providing ongoing feedback and by providing opportunities to learn through formal and informal methods		
Team Building		
Inspires and fosters team commitment, spirit, pride, and trust		
Facilitates cooperation and motivates team members to accomplish group goals		
HOW IMPORTANT IS YOUR ABILITY TO LEAD PEOPLE?		

EXECUTIVE CORE QUALIFICATION (ECQ) 3: RESULTS DRIVEN

1 = low 2 = medium 3 = high	1	2	3
Accountability			
Holds self and others accountable for measurable high-quality, timely, and cost-effective results			
Determines objectives, sets priorities, and delegates work			
Accepts responsibility for mistakes			
Complies with established control systems and rules			
Customer Service			
Anticipates and meets the needs of both internal and external customers			
Delivers high-quality products and services			
Is committed to continuous improvement			
Decisiveness			
Makes well-informed, effective, and timely decisions, even when data are limited or solutions produce unpleasant consequences			
Perceives the impact and implications of decisions			
Entrepreneurship			

Are You Happy

Positions the organization for future success by identifying new opportunities			
Builds the organization by developing or improving products or services			
Takes calculated risks to accomplish organizational objectives			
Problem Solving			
Identifies and analyzes problems			
Makes recommendations			
Weighs relevance and accuracy of information			
Generates and evaluates alternative solutions			
Technical Credibility			
Understands and appropriately applies principles, procedures, requirements, regulations, and policies related to specialized expertise			
HOW IMPORTANT IS YOUR ABILITY TO BE RESULTS DRIVEN?			

EXECUTIVE CORE QUALIFICATION (ECQ) 4: BUSINESS ACUMEN

1 = low 2 = medium 3 = high	1	2	3
Financial Management			
Understands the organization's financial processes			
Prepares, justifies, and administers the program budget			
Oversees procurement and contracting to achieve desired results			
Monitors expenditures and uses cost-benefit thinking to set priorities			
Human Capital Management			
Builds and manages the workforce based on organizational goals, budget considerations, and staffing needs			
Ensures that employees are appropriately recrulted, selected, appraised and rewarded			
Takes action to address performance problems			
Manages a multi-sector workforce and a variety of work situations			
Technology Management			
Keeps up-to-date on technological developments			

Finding the CEO in You

	1	2	3
Makes effective use of technology to achieve results			
Ensures access to and security of technology systems			
HOW IMPORTANT IS YOUR BUSINESS ACUMEN CAPABILITY?			
EXECUTIVE CORE QUALIFICATION (ECQ) 5: BUILDING COALITIONS			
1 = low 2 = medium 3 = high	1	2	3
Partnering			
Develops networks and builds alliances			
Collaborates across boundaries to build strategic relationships and achieve common goals			
Political Savvy			
Identifies the internal and external politics that impact the work of the organization			
Perceives organizational and political reality and acts accordingly			
Influencing/Negotiating			
Persuades others			
Builds consensus through give and take			
Gains cooperation from others to obtain information and accomplish goals			
HOW IMPORTANT IS YOUR ABILITY TO BUILD COALITIONS?			

How to interpret your results

1. Identify the ECQs that you rated *most important* for you (look for ratings of "3" for the last question in each section).

2. Scan that section for items that would make a significant difference to your outcomes. These could be low-rated items that you want to develop, or high-rated items that you want to use more.

Use the selected items to formulate goal statements that will best support your professional development over the next year.

CHAPTER 33
KEY SKILLS OF LEADERS AND SELF-ASSESSMENT

There is no exact definition of what a leader does. A leadership style is influenced by his or her personality and the challenges they face. If you search for the word leadership on Google, you will soon find out that there are many styles of leadership.

However, there are certain qualities that all good leaders share.

They are:
- Responsibility
- Awareness
- Confidence
- Decisiveness
- Empathy

Focus

Honesty
Inspiration
Optimism

Leadership plays a number of functions to ensure the smooth functioning of an organization. As you have seen in the previous chapter, the following skills are critical:

Strategic Thinking

One of the skills sought and expected of leaders in organizations is undoubtedly the ability to think, plan, and act strategically. This skill allows us to identify opportunities that will bring value to the

company; it also allows us to challenge the status quo and the premises on which the company is based to face current and future challenges. The absence of this competency will lead people to comply, to apply past solutions to future problems, to fail to identify threats as well as opportunities early on.

Inspiring and Motivating

An inspirational leader helps you bring out the best in yourself. A motivating leader pushes others' to do more and brings out the best in others. People who work for an inspiring leader are enthusiastic, encouraged, energized, motivated, and engaged.
They believe that what they do is essential and that they are making a difference.

Critical Thinking, Analyzing and Problem-Solving Abilities

Too often, we focus on the symptoms rather than the cause. When a leader is faced with a problem, he utilizes critical thinking and analyzes the problem finding solutions. A leader will identify the real issues underlying the symptoms by asking the right questions. Instead of stating the obvious (or the problem), the leader will provide ideas for solutions.

Are You Happy

Demonstrating Transparency, Integrity, and Honesty
To be successful in life, you have to be very honest because dishonesty always catches up with us. It is impossible to succeed

without developing a solid reputation for honesty and integrity. Interpersonal relationships are based on trust, and you cannot trust someone dishonest. As a leader, integrity is a crucial success factor, and the most critical persuasive tool a leader has. Honesty is the basis on which all other aspects are based. The leader is a model of integrity for others, and it's about being a role model to inspire others to behave similarly.

Developing Others
Great leaders are not afraid to recognize the skills of others and also support others in their development. A great leader realizes that it is essential to create an environment where exchange and knowledge transfer is a given. He truly believes that everybody has the opportunity to learn and grow.

Learning, Creating and Innovating
Not only are leaders supportive of others' learning, but they also thrive in learning new things. They love creating and innovating in their area of expertise. They are not afraid to say they don't know and learn about it. Leaders embrace changes as an opportunity to grow.

Driving Results
Leaders know how to drive results because their goal is clear, and they know how it relates to others. That is why they drive results because they know how to engage others in actions that will lead them to success. They understand how people are involved in the goal and find ways to spark that passion in others to move forward.

Communicating in a Powerful and Effective Way

Finding the CEO in You

It is one thing to know where you are going; it is another to be able to communicate it in a clear way that others understand you. A leader's communication is clear, open, and in alignment with their actions. The biggest communication tool a leader has is his behavior. What you see is what you get.

Building Relationships

It is believed that most leaders who are in a leadership role have acquired that role because of the relationship they have built. You are probably familiar with the following expression: "It is not what you know, but who you know." Knowing how to build relationships is vital if you want to be a strong leader. Not many people will follow a person they cannot relate to.

Displaying Technical or Professional Expertise

People look up to people who know things and can demonstrate skills and knowledge in their field. The same applies to leaders.

You can be a leader in your area if you are good at it. Others will look up to you for help when they struggle or advice to succeed like you.

Since leadership is not a natural skill for most of us, it becomes essential to be aware of where we lack and what we need to improve on. The following assessment will help you have an idea of your leadership skills and how much work you need to dedicate to your development.

Here are 14 questions that will help you define your leadership abilities.

1. Can you identify your three main strengths?

_____
_____
_____
_____

2. Can you identify your three main areas of concern?

_____

Are You Happy

3. Do your actions reflect your words and values?

4. Do you listen carefully to the ideas of those who disagree with you?

5. Are you bold enough to ask for feedback on your behaviors and use the information you gather as a tool to get to know yourself better?

6. When others do something wrong, do you take the time to help them see what they need to change and how they can solve problems?

7. Do you have the ability to assess the state of your environment and shape it to be better?

Finding the CEO in You

8. Do you have the ability to communicate a vision or goal?

9. Do you have the ability to mobilize people?

9. Do you have a propensity to encourage rather than criticize?

10. Do you have the ability to take risks?

11. Do you have a sense of innovation and creativity?

12. Do you have the ability to make decisions quickly?

13. Are you inspiring and admired by your employees?

14. Do you recognize your mistakes rather easily?

The number of "no" answers provide an indication of the various behaviors you could develop or reinforce to reach your ultimate potential as a leader. This book will help you do exactly that.

CHAPTER 34
LEADING WITHOUT THE TITLE

To become a great leader, you have to be a leader of your life. That is why you do not need a title to be a successful leader.

Before exploring this chapter any further, make a list of areas of your life where you are a leader, it could be as a parent, as a teammate, as a teacher or any other role that requires a certain amount of leadership.

I am a leader in the following areas of my life:

Finding the CEO in You

___

___

___

To be a leader means someone who is leading others, who holds a position of authority, or a responsibility. In summary, it is someone who has followers who look up to him or her. And yet, it is a particular fact that no one can, durably and with impact, guide others if he does not know how to conduct himself. Leading a group without a clear vision for oneself is a grave mistake that will lead you to inevitable failure.

Values

The starting point of personal leadership is your values; principles that you do not negotiate. They are an integral part of your being and even define you as a leader. These values are the foundation of your life.

Check all the values that are fundamental to you:

- Family
- Security
- Loyalty
- Intelligence
- Connection
- Creativity
- Humanity
- Success
- Respect
- Freedom
- Diversity
- Generosity
- Integrity
- Finesse
- Love
- Openness
- Honesty
- Kindness
- Teamwork
- Career
- Communication
- Learning
- Excellence
- Innovation
- Quality
- Adventure
- Contributing
- Spiritualism
- Strength
- Entertain
- Wealth
- Speed
- Courage
- Compassion
- Fitness
- Balance
- Relationship
- Knowledge
- Patience
- Change
- Prosperity
- Wellness
- Finances
- Gratitude
- Grace
- Endurance
- Facilitation
- Effectiveness

- Religion
- Power
- Fun

Are You Happy

- Order
- Affection
- Fame
- Advancement
- Cooperation
- Justice
- Respect
- Peace
- Appreciation
- Joy/Play
- Friendship/Relationship
- Willingness
- Forgiveness
- Encouragement
- Trusting Your Gut
- Work Smarter and Harder

- Pride in Your Work
- Giving People a Chance

- Excitement
- Clarity
- Patience
- Change
- Fun-Loving
- Forgiveness
- Goodness
- Charisma
- Self-Respect
- Involvement
- Humor
- Abundance
- Faith
- Leadership
- Reciprocity
- Wisdom
- Renewal
- Enjoyment
- Beauty
- Home
- Entrepreneurial
- Caring
- Be True
- Happiness

- Personal Development

- Contentment
- Harmony

Or any other values not listed above:

These values shape your reality, therefore your vision of the present world, your view of an ideal world. These values allow you to define yourself, to define your personality, and to position yourself clearly in your private or professional environment.

These values are most often linked to intrinsic qualities, qualities that are specific to you, that do not require much effort to be manifested; these qualities will be the foundation of your success. Knowing your intrinsic qualities increases your self-esteem.

Finding the CEO in You

Leadership is about leading to a goal, and personal leadership is about guiding you to your life goal. Moving away from your life goals would mean failure, but moving closer to it makes you shine brightly and reach your maximum potential.

Once your values and your qualities are known, once you have discovered your life purpose, you can take action. It is a matter of identifying all the activities necessary to achieve your life purpose. They will be grouped into objectives, i.e., groups of events that are coherent with each other and contribute to the same intermediate goal.

The objectives are essential to achieve your vision, without clearly defined missions, the vision would be only a wish. Once the mission has been chosen, it will allow you to focus on the essential and maximize the benefit of each effort.

Indeed, in the face of the multiple and diverse demands of life and others, it is essential to have a guideline which is the list of your critical missions to remain focused and, therefore, more effective.

This efficiency will allow you, day after day, to take one more step towards your life goal (or goals). Personal leadership means that you are fully responsible for reaching your life goal(s).

CHAPTER 35
LEAD YOURSELF TO SUCCESS WITH THE GROW MODEL

The best people to lead others in success are coaches. They are trained to do precisely that. One of the tools they use that is very efficient is called the GROW model.

What Is The GROW Model?

Finding the CEO in You

The GROW model is a simple and powerful coaching tool developed in the '80s by Graham Alexander, Alan Fine, and Sir John Whitmore. It is a straightforward four-step tool that is exceptionally intuitive and simple to put in action.

It is possible to use the GROW model on a personal goal or with a professional objective. Whatever the subject, whatever the problem, the mere existence of a solution to be found or a choice to be made can justify the four phases of the GROW model because it allows you to draw on your resources.

The GROW model's name is simply an acronym of the four steps, which are Goal, Reality, Options, and Will. Let's walk you through the steps.

GOAL (G)
We are going to start by identifying your goal or your objective. This can be the objective itself or the expected result. Be clear, concrete, and always focus on the target.

Here are some of the questions you can answer.

What do you want to accomplish in life?
_____
_____
_____
_____

Is there anything more important than this accomplishment?
_____
_____
_____
_____

How will you know that you have reached that goal?
_____
_____

Are You Happy

_____
_____

How does life look like when you have accomplished that goal?

_____
_____
_____

The goal should be specific enough to give you a direction. The objective can evolve during the various steps of the GROW model, but it should not be major unless it is an important lesson to learn.

REALITY (R)
In the reality phase, you will be describing the current situation and how is the current situation limiting you or empowering you to reach your goal. List the weaknesses and strengths you have for achieving this objective.

Here are some questions you can ask yourself in this phase:

How do I feel in regards to accomplishing my goal?

_____
_____
_____

What are the barriers to my goal?

_____
_____
_____

Finding the CEO in You

What are the values that are the most important right now?
_____
_____
_____
_____

What resources do I have to help me with my goal?
_____
_____
_____
_____

Am I resisting something in regards to my goal?
_____
_____
_____
_____

What limiting belief do I have in reaching my goal?
_____
_____
_____
_____

On a scale of 1 to 10 (1 being not at all, 10 being absolutely), how committed are you to that goal right now?
_____
_____
_____
_____

This phase will help you understand the situation and what led to it. It is useful to approach the situation from a cognitive, but especially emotional, perspective. This step uncovers the interferences (beliefs, objections, etc.) that oppose the achievement of the objective.

OPTIONS (O)

This step is essential. It is crucial to consider all options, including the most far-fetched ones. It is to know how to get out of standard solutions, being creative, innovating. Considering everything also makes it possible to rationally eliminate "halo," those inappropriate solutions that haunt us (ex: the magic pill that will lead you to weight loss).

Here are some questions you can ask yourself in this phase:

How can you be more committed to your goal?

___

How can you lift the barriers that limit you from reaching your goal?

___

If you had a magic wand, what option would you choose to realize your objective?

___

If you had more time, what would you do?

___

What if you could start all over, what would you do differently?

_____
_____
_____
_____

List all the possible actions to help you reach your goal.

_____
_____
_____
_____

This phase allows you to think of new opportunities to achieve your goal; What has not yet been done and which could contribute significantly to the achievement of the objective. It will help you support the implementation of behaviors, improvement of a process and modification of the time frame. It could even help with adopting a different position of perception. Brainstorm all the ideas that come to mind without judging them or limiting yourself. This phase is the time to dream.

WILL (W)

The last phase is about commitment and actions. It is the phase where you decide what you will do.

Here are some questions you can ask yourself in this phase:

Which option is your best and most actionable?

_____
_____
_____
_____

What is the first step or action?

_____
_____
_____

Are You Happy

When is your start date?

What else needs to happen?

On a scale of 1 to 10 (1 being not at all, 10 being absolutely), how committed are you to that first step now?

And how can you increase your score to be closer to 10?

How will you hold yourself accountable for that first step?

How will you know that you have completed the first step?

How will you celebrate your accomplishment of that first step?

_____
_____
_____
_____

The steps that will be made among the different options will involve a strong commitment to action that can produce change. This action may consist of doing nothing, changing a way of doing something, or a way to stop doing something. The important thing is to check the congruence of the commitment to action.

Once you have completed a cycle, go back to the option phase, and see if you can accomplish another action, repeat it until you reach your goal.

As you can see, the GROW model is adaptable and straightforward. It can take hours or the time of a coffee break. It is a perfect tool for taking a step back, and its regular use becomes quickly instinctive. In private life, the framework of the model allows you to assume your choices and often to identify them faster and more relevant.

~Thoughts~

_____
_____
_____
_____
_____
_____

Are You Happy

CHAPTER 36
SELF-AWARENESS AND PERSONAL GROWTH

The GROW model allows you to be aware of your goals, but there is another type of awareness that is critical in leadership: Self-awareness.

Self-awareness also means developing the ability to know oneself as a leader. Learning to spot what is going on inside us when we are stressed and under pressure, when we are on the autopilot or when our mental chatter takes up all the space and cuts us off from the direct experience of the present moment and the possibilities of being proactive.

We now know very well how harmful chronic stress is to both physical and psychological health. It might not be well known, but the stress we carry overwhelms those around us. In the workplace, this information is of prime importance because it has a direct effect on the quality of leadership.

Our brain is designed for survival, and it continually scans our environment for potential threats. Thus, any perceived threat (real or relative stress) then triggers the secretion of stress hormones. The body and mind are then in a state of alert. What happens when a leader is stressed by too much pressure? The brain of people around the leader instinctively perceives it as a threat, and the leader then becomes a potential danger. Concretely, their ability to think, make good decisions, and be creative will be reduced to its simplest expression, or worse, may become inaccessible.

Mindfulness, therefore, teaches leaders to be proactive, to recognize the signs of stress as soon as they appear so that they can respond appropriately to keep them healthy and maintain team cohesion through mobilizing leadership. Self-awareness allows the leader to become aware of automatisms. The automatic pilot is the mental program that opens the door to behaviors that are deeply rooted over time, such as habits, prejudices, narrow perceptions, or ruminations.

These automatisms, which keep us within the framework of what we know and which we unconsciously reproduce despite ourselves, limit innovation, lead to the repetition of negative experiences and block the ability to change. Learning how to recognize them and how to flush them out is of primary importance for the leader.

Self-awareness allows us to recognize the mental chatter that leads us through a maze of thoughts and opinions rather than keeping in touch with direct experience. We mistakenly believe that what this inner discourse tells us must be accurate, but experts in neurology tell us that it is more like a brain cleanse. Moreover, it cuts the leader off from all available relevant information obtained through active listening and authentic communication with others.

Cultivating self-awareness means developing the ability to observe yourself with patience and benevolence to get to know yourself and recognize your ways of functioning as a leader to transform them. It is the fundamental foundation on which other skills and qualities can be built to ensure the well-being of yourself and those around you.

Mindfulness meditation is the training of the mind. It is the gym of the brain that invariably brings us back into the present moment away from unconscious programs to develop self-awareness.

This transformation is possible because our brain can transform and reshape itself as a result of daily training. Building on this capacity means encouraging the adoption of new leadership skills that are better adapted to the mobilization of teams and the human management of resources.

CHAPTER 37
BE AN INSPIRING AGENT OF CHANGE

Finding the CEO in You

Being an agent of change is not a natural role, especially when you have to go against the grain of the culture or the established behaviors and comfort zones of the people around you. However, it is something that does not scare leaders.

Changes, as a whole, comes with a lot of resistance, but only patience will overcome it. As a leader, you have to learn to embrace change and see it with the mindset of growth instead of a threat.

Humans are rarely open to changing their lifestyle or habits since their comfort zone has been carefully established. In other words, during the years, they have been with their family, their spouse, their colleague, and their friends, they have adapted their behavior to the needs of the moment.

No matter if the change you want to make is at work, at home, or in your social life, it will likely impact others.

To be an inspiring change agent, you must support and show compassion toward others. Nothing is accepted radically or by forcing the transition. Keeping an open communication with the people who are impacted by the change is critical. Regularly inform people before, during, and after the change. Reassure the people involved by allowing them to contribute to the change.

In time of change, the principle is simple: lead by example. As an agent of change, you must become what you want others to become. You need to set an example, and you are one. Every word you say, every behavior you are responsible for, will have an impact on the community as a whole.

Change is something we experience every day in our daily lives. Even if we believe in a routine, our lives are continually changing. Change has allowed us to reinvent our lives and our living environment since the dawn of time.

~Thoughts~

Are You Happy

CHAPTER 38
BARRIERS TO LEADERSHIP

"With great power comes great responsibility"…and significant barriers. It is essential to be aware that leadership is not an easy skill to acquire. There are many barriers that you may come across during your development as a leader.

Here are a few to help you be aware of them.

Being Open to Feedback
Even when we feel that criticism is unfair and subjective, it is best to open up and learn from it. Here are three ways for responding to feedback proposed by the Harvard Business Review:

Don't react immediately: Feedback should not be dismissed when given. By being calm and respectful, you allow the space for the feedback to be heard. Most people who provide feedback has a good intention, the intention being to improve something. You might not agree with the opinion, but it might trigger a good thinking process.

Understand the feedback: Since the objective of constructive feedback is to improve. It is essential to understand what we are being asked to correct. Make the other person feel heard by asking questions to clarify their point and bring some insight into the reason behind the feedback. You can use an old trick by therapists, which is to rephrase what you have heard to make sure it is understood clearly.

Don't let it get to you: It might come across as you are the problem, or the problem is directly connected to one of your behavior. If that is the case, don't let personal criticism get to you and your confidence. Use the information to help you grow and let go of what you cannot control (such as people's opinion of you).

Moving Into Action

Many will get stuck in the planning mode, implementing a change or an action is harder than it looks. Do not get stuck in the planning and make sure that you take small steps or actions, every day, toward your goal. Another aspect that will stop you from moving into action is getting stuck in the busy pace of life.

Not having time is an excuse for not taking action; the reason is that you did not make your goal a priority.

Accepting Responsibility for Mistakes

Leadership comes at a price, the spotlight is often on you, and if you do not accept the responsibility of your mistakes, people will notice it. If you want to be a great leader, you need to be a role model and show others that it is OK to make mistakes. Mistakes do not define who you are; they define who you were and allow you to grow and become a better version of yourself.

Facing Disagreement

Learn to embrace conflict and disagreement in a way that you do not take it personally. Leaders thrive in conflict because they know that any conflict will bring growth and improvement. Conflict resolution might be one of the most challenging aspects of relationships, but when you learn to be comfortable with them, you do not run away when they happen.

Confidence When Facing Failure

Failures are imminent when you are trying something new or trying to change. It might be a big or a small failure. As a leader, you need to see failure as an opportunity to learn why it did not work and what needs to change. As Thomas A. Edison sophisticatedly said: "I have not failed. I have just found 10,000 ways that won't work."

Maintaining Focus

As a leader, it is often very easy to be distracted. You need to figure out ways to stay on track to your goal and reduce all the distractions that stir you away from your accomplishment.

Because you will be known to be a problem solver, you will be consistently interrupted by others to help them with their problem. Find ways to empower others to be leaders in their life and remove some of the tasks you do for them.

Humility Versus Success

When you become popular or successful as a leader, humility can quickly disappear from your qualities. While humility is essential in great leaders, you can make sure that you do not lose it by always being aware of others and their contribution. Be a collaborative member of society and remain in integrity with who you are and where you are going.

Learn When to Step Aside

Leaders may often be seen as being in front of the pack, but like Simon Sinek's latest book title, "Leaders eat last." That is a lesson we can learn from great military leaders. Allowing others to lead the group, or the goal, is good and mostly very motivating to the group. Be aware that you do not always have to come up with solutions or ideas; allow the space to get help from others.

Now that we have talked about the barriers to leadership let's explore the blueprint that will lead you to become a successful leader for all aspects of your life.

~Thoughts~

Are You Happy

Chapter 39

BLUEPRINT TO DEVELOP YOUR LEADERSHIP SKILLS

In this chapter, we list ways that you can develop your leadership skills through two fundamental abilities, which are mindfulness and courage.

Practice mindfulness
According to Jon Kabat-Zinn, mindfulness is: "Being able to pay direct and open attention to what one is doing at the moment one is doing it, in a non-judgmental conscious way." Mindfulness is also an invitation to get out of the autopilot responses, reactions, and habits that push us towards movements of impatience, lack of listening, or even indifference towards others.

A leader is not a perfect or heroic being, but by the charisma and self-confidence, he exudes one wants to be like him. The qualities of a good leader are recognized in his vision of the future and his pursuit of excellence. Credible and with integrity while possessing deep respect for others, he has developed his emotional intelligence and knows how to demonstrate flexibility and open- mindedness. You can feel all the authenticity in him. Mindfulness brings additional skills that act as a catalyst for the leader and allow him to easily bring people in a collaborative mode while stimulating their creativity.

Are You Happy

Inspired by Ellen Choi and Michael Rouse, here are four characteristics that distinguish Mindfulness Leaders and allow them to have an impact on the effectiveness of their teams:

Their vigilance and attention: Contrary to the belief that persists, full presence does not make you nonchalant or amorphous. On the contrary, it allows you to develop a quality of alertness and an unparalleled capacity for focus. While having a precise vision of the objectives to be achieved, open attention in the present moment allows one to seize opportunities as they arise, and to adjust the focus when necessary.

Self-awareness: Self-awareness allows the leader to develop an awareness of his physical, mental, and emotional state. He learns to recognize what is going on inside him.

Self-regulation: Self-regulation provides control to achieve one's goals. By developing the ability to keep focus and attention in a particular direction for a specific period of time, productivity and performance are increased while reducing mental fatigue and the risk of errors.

Transcendence of self to understand the other: Self-transcendence is the ability to consider the needs of others and to choose the course of action that reflects the best interests of a larger group of people. This ability to make appropriate and informed choices is essential to ensure the sustainability of the business, and it promotes positive and satisfying relationships with the team and the organization.

Here are two activities that will help you practice mindfulness and become a better leader.

Exercise 1: Breathing Consciously

Regularly during the day, take short breaks between tasks, and take a few seconds just to breathe. You stop everything you are doing 30, 20, or even 5 seconds and concentrate only on your breathing.

When you practice mindfulness breathing, you forget what you were doing, what you are going to do next, and you focus only on your breath. You are just observing the air come in and watching the air go out. You feel your belly inflation with air and then deflation. You visualize the path of the air when you inhale and when you exhale. And as soon as you become aware that you are giving energy to a thought, then smile and slowly return to your breathing. Try it now.

Stop reading and take a few conscious breaths. Or just one. Stop what you were doing and take a deep breath in and out. Put all your attention on it, not only your lungs breathing, but your whole body. Every cell in your body stops and enjoys that breath.

Practice this exercise many in your day, and you will soon realize that you are more mindful of your breath throughout the day.

Exercise 2: Walking with awareness

During a walk, a stroll, or even at home, you can also practice mindfulness by walking. Be fully present during your walk. It does not matter where you go. It does not matter where you come from, either. Observe every step and how they feel.

Every step is a destination in itself. With each step, you can try to feel the sensation of your foot touching the ground. First, you will feel the heel touching the ground, then the rest of the foot. You can also slow down your walk a little to be present with each step. Try to act as if you were hugging the ground with each step. Be as gentle as possible with every step on the ground.

Everything can become an exercise in mindfulness. Every action of daily life can be transformed into mindfulness meditation if it is lived fully. Every task in everyday life can be mindfulness training: whether it is gardening, washing dishes, or driving a car.

Whatever the situation is, it is simply a matter of being more present to what we are doing and devoting our full attention to it. Living life with a clear conscience is simply living life, and it will help you become a great leader and, mostly, an inspiring leader.

Practice Courage

We all need a strong leader who knows how to make difficult decisions, who knows how to protect others and stay the course in difficult times.

A good leader does not give up at the first difficulty encountered: he accepts failures as tests and knows that the path to the goal is not a long, calm river. In the face of adversity, the leader must sharpen up, show even more determination to reach the goal, and must have learned from his mistakes.

You know it as well as I do: before committing ourselves behind someone, we always wait to see their courage, their determination, their perseverance. A group of people will be much more willing to show courage if their leader sets an example. But how does one become courageous? Here are

Step 1: Admit That You Are Afraid

Being brave does not mean that you are not afraid; it means you can move forward no matter how scared you are. If you try to push your emotions away, they will only get stronger. You have to recognize that fear is present. Identify your fears, consciously.

You do not have to tell anyone else, just yourself.

Step 2: Accept Your Fear

Your emotions are normal and neutral. It is the feeling that we are attached to the emotion that becomes good or bad. You will not help yourself by judging yourself on this emotion, and you will not become braver. It can be helpful to read stories of people who have faced their fears. It can help you understand that you are not alone in your fear and help you to accept that fear more quickly.

Step 3: Observe Your Fears

Take the role of the observer and observe your emotion. We are afraid when we perceive a situation as being wrong. Some fears are legitimate, but others are very irrational. Observe your fear and decide if it is logical or something you can move forward with.

Step 4: Be Vulnerable

Accept everything as a risk. Try not to see things in terms of failures or successes, but as experiences that you can learn from. Uncertainty is the source of many fears. You can learn to tolerate risk by working it out little by little in your daily life.

Step 5: Surrender

Certain things in life cannot be controlled, such as the future. There is no way that you could know the future with certainty. Let go of the need to control the outcome and simply live in the present moment. Remember that you cannot control the outcome of a situation. You can only control what you do. Instead, focus on your actions, not the results.

Step 6: Find an Inspiration

Find a role model, and it could be someone you know or a famous leader. If they are close to you, or accessible, ask them how they faced their fears. Try to copy the behavior of someone who has faced adversity. And do not forget, you can always ask for help.
Others can be a great source of courage when they hold our hands during something scary.

Step 7: Be Resilient

Resilience is the ability to face adversity, and, in some ways, it is a form of courage. Courage requires resistance in the face of a frightening or painful situation. Work on your ability not to become a victim and to find new ways to approach a problem or situation. You need to deal with it. Courageous people look at the situation and identify a way to approach it, rather than trying to ignore the problem. Things are not always going to be easy or straightforward. Resilient people understand this and get up after they fall.

Step 8: Nothing Is Perfect.

It is often believed that perfectionism is the same as ambition. In reality, the desire for perfection is responsible for fear paralysis. We may be paralyzed by fear and stop all efforts to accomplish our goals. This prevents us from experiencing loss or failure, which is not possible in life. The quest for perfection can make you so hard on yourself. Focus on the process rather than the outcome.

Step 9: Try Something Difficult

You might feel more confident in achieving something you found insurmountable. Think of this challenge as an opportunity to learn and remember that you can take the time you want to learn. Find ways to set goals and challenge yourself. Courage is not always visible. Sometimes having courage just means standing up and trying again.

Step 10: Train Yourself to Be Conscious

Practice conscious, non-judgmental acceptance techniques (like the one above) to help you accept negative and positive emotions. Mindfulness meditation is an excellent way to examine your fears and give you more courage.

Step 11: Create a Plan

It is easy to get scared when you do not know what to do. Consider the possible obstacles that could stand in your way. Think about all the obstacles you might face and create a plan of action. All of a sudden, your fear of the unknown will be irrelevant since you have a plan and know how it will move forward.

Are You Happy

~Thoughts~

CHAPTER 40
BEING A GOOD LEADER TO BECOMING A GREAT LEADER

There are a few qualities that will make you move from a good leader to a great leader. The essential qualities are the following:

Self-confidence: Developing your self-confidence is essential to be able to give confidence to others and communicate your vision and ideas effectively.

Vision: Not only do leaders have a goal, but they also have a vision where many goals can take place in the long term.

Open-mindedness: Be open to learning; no one holds the truth. Knowing how to question oneself and remaining curious about any new opportunity or possibility is essential to make a dream come true. The leader knows that alone, he cannot achieve much. Unity, and therefore collective intelligence, is strength.

Exemplarity: This is a fundamental principle. To be listened to and followed, one must set an example and apply oneself to what one preaches.

Are You Happy

Consistency is one's values and convictions: A great leader will not be able to convince himself if he is not genuinely in agreement with the project and the ideas he defends.

Multidisciplinary intelligence: A good leader instinctively senses what his collaborators are capable of, but also their personality and way of working. With this in mind, he can orchestrate his world and lead it to the best possible success for everyone.

Empathy: An integral part of a developed emotional intelligence that enables the leader to get the best out of each person by allowing them to develop fully.

Freedom: Independence of thoughts and action is intimately correlated with self-confidence and a sense of responsibility.

Responsibility: Linked to the previous point, the leader, free in his choices, must take responsibility for his decisions, risk-taking, and mistakes.

In addition to the qualities detailed below, a great leader must know:

Take the initiative: This is often where the great leader is admired and respected because he is determined, confident, and daring.

Defend and impose his ideas gently and respectfully: What is the point of having good ideas if one is not able to present them in a respectful and courteous nonviolent way? Knowing how to convince is, consequently, a significant asset.

Communicate effectively: An essential skill to get your ideas across and o win the support of your troops. Feedback is an integral part of this, as it allows the leader to remain attentive to his collaborators, to hear new possibilities and opportunities, etc.

Recognize the talents of others: One of the pillars of leadership, which consists of identifying, developing, and orchestrating individual and collective skills to lead everyone to success.

Invite change and innovation: Disruption and innovation are two dominant notions in leadership. They allow you to continually question your ideas, your work, and the entire group to reach the heights you dream of.

Motivate and recognize others: A great leader must also manage his troops, and play on motivation and meaning at work, to maintain his position as an ongoing leader.

Are You Happy

~Thoughts~

Finding the CEO in You

As you have seen in this book, leadership is a state of mind and not a position in an organization. Therefore, being a leader is, above all, a state of mind. It is the ability to put into action their ambitions and objectives while staying the course and leading others to a common goal.

It also means having courage. Mastering one's strengths and weaknesses to make them pillars of your daily actions and to inspire others. Accept yourself and accept all life challenges around you. By doing so, you will realize that in so many ways, you are already a leader in your life.

Be mindful that leadership is not a skill that we develop overnight, it takes time and effort, and it is, in many ways, the constant development of skills. As a leader, there will always be a moment of doubt or a complex problem that you cannot figure out. That is why it is so essential to build a support group around you. Find people that are there to support you when you need them and vice-versa.

Great leaders are always surrounded by amazing people who do not hesitate to step forward and lead the leader in a difficult time.

Continue being open to learning new things, explore the world around you, and be humble; you will see that others will respect you for it. And most of all, be yourself. Integrity and authenticity are always admired in leaders that are not afraid to be themselves and embrace who they truly are, flaws and all.

Everyone has had the experience of working for a not-so-great boss. While it's common for people to be promoted into management when they excel in non-leadership positions, the truth is that a lot of the people who get those promotions don't have the skills they need to effectively manage their team.

In other words, they lack the must-have leadership skills that all great bosses have in common.

The good news is that they're skills you can easily learn. In this special report, I'll explain the five essential leadership skills you need to successfully manage a team, and how to set yourself up for long-term success.

These critical steps include: communication, adaptability, team building, strategic thinking, and delegation.

Are you ready to learn what it takes to become an effective leader? Let's get started!

Skill 1: Communication

Without proper, clear and concise communication, you can't hope to become an effective leader.

Communication is your best tool for explaining your ideas, setting expectations, and building your team. In this chapter, we'll talk about why strong communication skills are essential for leaders and share some tips about how to communicate effectively both in writing and in person.

The Importance of Interpersonal Communication

Interpersonal communication is what builds relationships. If you listen to employees complain about their bosses and employers, one of the top issues they're dealing with is usually lack of a direct and clear channel of communication.

Of course, communication goes both ways. But, as a leader, it's your job to set the tone for interaction within your organization or team.

Effective communication:

    Minimizes misunderstandings and confusion
    Ensures that team members know what you expect
    Encourages communication among team members
    Increases the chances that you'll reach your goals

Any time you touch base with your team or with a client, you're using communication skills. That means every phone call, every meeting, every chat, and every email reflects your ability to communicate and keep a pulse on how projects are going.

Tips for Effective Communication in Writing and Off the Cuff

What makes for effective communication? The hallmarks of a good communication are clarity, detail, and honesty.

Clarity means that you must be able to articulate what you want in a way that the person you're talking to can understand. You're not communicating effectively if the listener or reader can't understand what you need or expect from them.

Detail means that you are specific about what you want, expect, or need to know. If you delegate a task and the team member still has questions about what to do or how to do the job, your communication skills have fallen short.

Honesty means that you must be truthful when communicating with your team. That doesn't mean you need to tell them everything you're thinking all the time, but it does mean that you cannot mislead them or deliberately omit information that might help them achieve the goals you've laid out for the team.

Are You Happy

Here are a few tips for communicating effectively:

- In writing, keep your sentences and paragraphs short
- Think about what you say before you say it
- Always keep your audience in mind. Don't use jargon unless you're sure they'll understand it
- Pay attention to how the listener reacts to what you say
- Be available to answer questions and patient while you do it

These tips will help you be an effective communicator and enhance your ability to lead.

Coming up next, we'll talk about why you must be adaptable if you want to become a great leader.

Business Communication

1. Also called barriers. Numerous factors that hinder the communication process.

2. A type of communication that is generally a response to requests from supervisors.

3. People inside and outside the organization who are affected by decisions.

4. The study of how a culture perceives time and its use.

5. A situation in which the whole is greater than the sum of its parts.

6. The ability to read, empathize and

A. Extranet

B. Norm

C. Lateral Report

D. Casual Listening

E. Analytical Report

F. Interferences

understand others.

7. Listening for pleasure, recreation, amusement and relaxation.	G. Synergy
8. A standard or average behavior.	H. Brainwashing
9. A team that brings together employees from various departments to solve a variety of problems.	I. Inductive
10. Stage four of team development in which team members reach the optimal performance level.	J. Persuasive Requests
11. The generation of many ideas from among team members.	K. Interpersonal Intelligence
12. Written defamatory remarks.	L. Stakeholders
13. Spoken defamatory remarks	M. Persuasion
14. A message in which the major idea follows the details.	N. Performing
15. When the subject of a sentence is the doer of an action.	O. Secondary Research
16. Specialized terminology that professionals in some fields use when communicating with colleagues in the same field.	P. Libel
17. A kind word substituted for one that may offend or suggest something unpleasant.	Q. Cross Functional Team
18. The buzzword for proper behavior on the internet.	R. Proposal
19. Web platform for distributing information to business partners such as	S. Informal Report

vendors and customers.

20. Messages that assume that requested information will be taken after persuasive arguments are presented.
T. Upward Communication

21. The ability of a sender to influence others to accept his or her point of view.
U. Euphamism

22. Usually a short message written in natural or personal language.
V. Netiquette

23. A report that presents suggested solutions to problems.
W. Chronemics

24. A report that travels between units on the same organizational level.
X. Slander

25. A written description of how one organization can meet the needs of another.
Y. Jargon

26. Provides information that has already been reported by others.
Z. Active Voice

Skill 2: Adaptability

You've heard about survival of the fittest. It's the principle that tells us that only those who can handle change and cope with adversity survive. In other words, adaptability is necessary – and it can mean the difference between success and failure in your business.

In this chapter, we'll talk about why great leaders must be adaptable, and provide some tips about how you can increase your adaptability and learn to go with the flow.

How Adaptability Can Help You Succeed

Finding the CEO in You

In our professional lives, things seldom go the way we want them to. There are too many variables for that to always be the case and often, the things that derail our career or our personal lives feels as though it's out of our control.

There have been many times in my life when I've had an expectation that hasn't been met – and I'm willing to bet that's true for you, too.

The bottom line is that what you do in the face of adversity is what will determine whether you're able to quickly recover, reset and get back on the path to success.

If you have a setback, do you get up and keep going – or do you give up and move onto something else?

Great leaders learn to go with the flow. They understand that success doesn't happen overnight. Their adaptability helps them get through failure and come out the other side a winner.

Tips for Increasing Adaptability and Going with the Flow

Some people have a high level of adaptability naturally. If that's you, then you're probably in good shape.

But what if it's not? What if you're easily discouraged or daunted by setbacks? Is there anything you can do to increase your adaptability?

Yes!

Here are some tips to help you increase your adaptability and go with the flow.

1. Make contingency plans. You should always have a Plan B. It doesn't mean you're planning for failure. Instead, it means that you've given thought to what you'll do if Plan A doesn't go as planned.

2. Practice resilience. If you're like most people, you probably experience tons of small setbacks. When one happens, pay attention to how you react and think about how you can switch up your internal monologue to be more positive.

3. Come up with a daily affirmation to remind yourself that you can deal with disappointment. You might try something like, "Even if things don't go my way today, I'm going to keep going and not get bogged down by it."

4. When something goes wrong, don't react immediately. Take a few deep breaths and let yourself feel the disappointment. A lot of times, we get wrapped up in disappointment because we're trying to hard to overcome it. It's okay to feel disappointed – but it's not okay to let it get the best of you.

These tips can help you learn to be more resilient. Even a big disappointment or a disappointing failure doesn't have to mean that your goals are out of reach.

Coming up next, we'll talk about how to build a team – something that's very important for every leader. Keep reading to learn more!

Skill 3: Team Building

We'll always reach a higher level of success with a team. Even the self-made millionaires and billionaires out there didn't do it entirely on their own. Bill Gates is a great example. Yes, he had a great idea when he created Windows – but he had a talented team of programmers, designers, writers, marketers, and administrators to help him launch it.

In this chapter, we'll talk about why team-building is an essential leadership skill, and how you can recognize the areas where you need help so you can build a powerhouse team of your own.

The Benefits of Building a Strong Team

As hard as you may work and as determined as you may be, you can't do everything on your own, nor should you. It's not practical, and it's not working smarter – it's working harder.

Consider the phrase, "Jack of all trades, master of none." You might be great at some things, but chances are there are areas in your business that would benefit from outside support.

You might be tempted to try to do everything yourself, telling yourself that you'll save money. A lot of entrepreneurs make that mistake and it leads to failure. They undervalue their time and energy and underestimate how hard it will be to wear every hat, every day.

Choosing a team means that you'll have ongoing support within your own customized network. You can delegate tasks – something we'll talk about later – and have time to do the things you do best. You'll also be able to enjoy other aspects of life because, let's face it, you'll work better if you make time to play, too.

The trick, of course, is building the right team.

Tips for Attracting Team Members and Knowing When You Need Help

You need a team, but where you do you start?

The first step is identifying the key areas where you need help. If you're building a business, you'll need to build a brand, create products, design your website, structure mailing lists, attract new clients, service those clients, and so on.

Start by looking at the things you do very well. Maybe you're a killer salesperson or a master communicator. Those may be things you can do on your own.

Are You Happy

Next, look at the things that aren't in your wheelhouse. Maybe you have very little marketing experience or you're not great at organization.

The first team members you hire should be the people who can help you with your weaknesses. You'll have the best chance of success if you use this method.

The next thing you need to do is attract the right team members.

To do that, you'll need to:

Write accurate and attractive job descriptions.
Offer fair payment.
Place ads to help team members find you or look for them on sites like LinkedIn.
Interview people.

Make sure that you ask for samples of their work where it's appropriate and check their references. These days, it's easy to hire people to work remotely without ever meeting them. You should set up Skype interviews with anyone you don't plan to meet in person.

It's also a good idea to impose a probation period on any new hires. That way, you'll be able to make changes easily if you need to. Just make sure to put everything in writing.

Next, we'll talk about strategic thinking.

Team Building

```
I O S D F S M O P X P T G E X Q W W K M N W O E
A A I F F U O J L I I J X M W A K X E V R Z V T
W Q N Y J F H Y T O H N F A A G K T R I O F W A
W I L C V K M Z E O R S F Z N D S B C A T I T I
G Y C F P T Q C U T O A R I B Y N Q V J C N W C
```

Finding the CEO in You

```
K R O W M A E T P U S N T O S W H A L D E A T O
R G F X F N K B B T T C E T T Y J G N O R N C S
G E B I C T D I S V E Y A F I N W N G K I C W S
W A C B R B G T Q P T M U G J C E G M N D I J A
M O E R I E A D S X R S G N E J C M A R G A B I
E T G I U R B O D O C N O O K I I N Q U N L U Q
O X A S T I R A F W I V E I M F M D A W I N I M
G G R R W P T S L S A B A T A L X X D F T E L U
V I E X U C S I N L U R D O C S M X C U E E D T
D N V C Z E G E N U D Y C M C O H W C E K D I N
E H E O N U C Y O G U H A O V R H O R F R S N E
Z R L I Z I S L B N K O Y R A Y M P G L A A G M
F M S C L E L I P X Y D H P V P F I N F M N P O
J U E H C A O R P P A B P E L O K W I J R A B M
B X U T P D N C K O X Y T I J V R W T B O L D L
I K A G S E I R E D A R A M A C X L I G I Y I Q
B P I Z O Y A J T G M N M O S X B A V M N S T J
A M T Z Y E S W O G C Q J A M E F I N Z E I C U
N Y L Z M I J W S E R S Q A D F S S I K S S X J
```

SENIOR MARKETING DIRECTOR   FINANCIAL NEEDS ANALYSIS   BUSINESS FORMAT SYSTEM   CAMARADERIE   PROSPECTING   COMPLIANCE   MENTORSHIP   FAST START   RECRUITING   PROMOTION   LICENSING   ASSOCIATE   TEAMWORK   BUILDING   APPROACH   INVITING   FIREBALL   MOMENTUM   LEVERAGE   SYSTEM

Skill 4: Strategic Thinking

Strategy thinking is an essential element of leadership. In this chapter, I'll explain why and give you some tips for improving your strategic thinking and planning skills.

Are You Happy

The Role of Strategy in Success

Strategy is simply long-term planning with a fancy name. You have a goal in mind and then you map out a step-by-step plan to achieve it. If you want it to work, your strategy must be logical and practical. Each step you take should build to the next step.

Without strategy, it's very difficult – maybe even impossible – to achieve your biggest goals. You might have the goal to be the CEO of a Fortune 500 company. Your strategy might include getting an MBA and a host of other steps that will put you in a position to achieve that goal.

The thing about strategy is that it's not just for you. Having a strategy in place can help you get investors to fund your company, and it can also help you inspire your team.

Tips for Improving Your Strategic Thinking and Planning Ahead

Some people have a natural gift for strategic thinking. They're the people who are great chess players and who naturally seem to see everything 10 steps ahead.

If you're not one of them, don't worry. Here are some tips to help you improve your strategic thinking.

Before you make any decision, think about some possible outcomes and brainstorm what you'll do next with each one. This is the kind of practical thinking that can help you become a better strategist.

Think about your goals and work backwards to figure out what actions will help you achieve them. Think of this as reverse-engineering a strategy.

Ask team members and trusted friends for suggestions to help you plan strategically.

Try creating a timeline to plan each step on the way to your goal.

The more you practice strategic thinking, the easier it will be.

Coming up next, we'll talk about the fifth and final must-have leadership skill in this book: delegation.

Thinking Strategies: Size of Problem, Inner Coach, Flexibility

1. TCNIEEPA INEATPCE PNETIACE

___

2. SI SHTI HET EBTS HEOCIC

___

3. TAWH ARE UYOR PNITOSO

___

4. LLI' TGE TRUHGOH SHIT

___

5. E'IV OEDN STIH FEREBO

___

6. NOE ESTP TA A EITM

___

7. TPOS NDA IHTNK

___

8. NOT A BGI EALD

___

9. YOU NAC OD IT

___

10. BE LXEBLEIF

___

Skill 5: Delegation

In some ways, delegation is the most important skill of them all. I've already touched on some reasons why it's important not to try to do everything yourself. The key to making that happen is to learn how to delegate effectively.

In this chapter, we'll talk about why delegation is important and provide some tips to help you delegate the right tasks to the right people.

Why You Shouldn't Try to Do Everything Yourself

Finding the CEO in You

If you want to be a great leader, you need to know how to delegate tasks and – just as importantly – who to delegate them to.

You might have a ton of energy and the will to do everything yourself, but as I said before, it's not always an effective strategy. Not only will you be shouldering the responsibility for tasks that aren't in your wheelhouse, but you also run the risk of burning out.

We all need down time – and we all do our best work when we're focused on what we're good at and love to do. Delegation allows you to focus your time and energy on the things you're best it and the things that only you can do.

That means you'll have more time to lead because you won't be burned out from trying to do everything.

Tips to Help You Decide What to Delegate to Others

The trick to great delegation is knowing two things:

1. Which tasks and jobs can be delegated; and
2. Who should handle those tasks.

So, let's take each of these things in turn, starting with knowing which tasks to delegate. You should delegate:

- Things that your team members excel at
- Things they can be taught to do
- Things that don't require your personal input

It might be useful to start by identifying the things that only you can do. These may include making strategic decisions about your team or meeting with investors.

Then, make a list of the things you can delegate. Once you've got the list, it's time to think about who the best people are for those jobs. Here are some questions to ask:

Which team members already have skills that make them suitable for the task?

Are You Happy

Which team members have shown aptitude for core skills, like communication, teamwork, or logic?

Which team members are eager to learn and willing to take on something new?

Any of these questions can help you identify people who are ready to handle the tasks and responsibilities you've identified.

Once you've identified the people you need, you should spend some time thinking about the training and support they'll need to succeed with their delegated tasks. You may need to spend some one-on-one time with them or pay someone else to train them. They may need an outside class or seminar.

Delegate the tasks, and make sure that you communicate clearly and in detail about what you expect from each team member.

Make yourself available to answer questions, and most importantly, keep in mind that they may not get it right on the first try.

There's a chance that you may need to adapt along the way. You might not pick the best team member for every task on your first try. The key is to keep an open mind, listen, and be patient.

You'll need all your leadership skills to decide what to delegate, choose the best people for each job, and guide them along the way to success. That's why I saved delegation for last – because it's a skill that necessarily incorporates all the others we've discussed.

Final Words

As a reminder, here are some core concepts to remember as you work to build your leadership skills:

Finding the CEO in You

1. Practice communication all the time and be willing to learn from your mistakes. Remember that all communication should be done with clarity, detail, and honesty.
2. Improve your adaptability by reminding yourself that you can handle disappointment and by learning to make contingency plans.
3. Build your team by recognizing the danger of trying to do everything yourself and choosing team members who have the skills and experience you lack.
4. Learn how to think strategically by outlining your goals and identifying the practical steps you need to take to achieve them.
5. Delegate skills by assigning the tasks that don't require your personal attention to the team members best suited to do them.

Some so-called experts treat leadership like it's a riddle to be solved. I don't think of it that way. It's a skill – or rather a set of skills – that anybody can acquire if they're willing to do the work.

The five core skills I've described in this book can be the basis of great leadership. I believe you can be a great leader – and you should too!

Management & Delegation

```
M C M A N A G E M E N T O T N U T
E F F E C T I V E A W N D A P V I
E T T E A M W O R K N I O A T S M
C C B B B J V A T C X Y T Z Y A E
```

Are You Happy

```
I E N C O J B H L B N I J O U A M
T P C O C O D E O F E T H I C S A
C S N O I T A I C N U M M O C I N
A E B J V T Z I T J A P M J C Z A
R R Z C O L A S Z S D P J W S S G
P I Q Z L M A G S P E A H G C F E
F E S O R F N I E T L U R D I R M
O B K R E A G D E L N M A G R P E
E M Y T X N L N A E E Q D H W W N
P G Y N M L T N N N F D I Z I E T
O L V E A K R F V I R O O V G U N
C E N C I A U S E I T I R O I R P
S T Z Q C F D T N E D I F N O C U
```

Scope of Practice   Time Management   Code
of Ethics   Patient Safety   Communciation
Assignment   Delegation   Management
Priorities   Competent   Confident

Effective   New Grad   Teamwork

Finding the CEO in You

Respect   CARNA

Are You Happy

Extras:

Being wealthy does not have to be difficult if you have the know-how. In these hard economic times many people are satisfied by just getting by and scraping enough money together to pay the bills.

Wealth and financial freedom are a far-off dream for many people. For them, it means mansions, gated communities, a fast car, private parties or a pool. The truly wealthy have family names like Rockefeller or Morgan.

It can be easy to accumulate wealth. The thing is, not everyone knows how. The twentieth century has bought a boom of first-time millionaires, many of which do not come from family money. They make their first million by employing timeless wealth wisdom and secrets only the ultra rich used to know. Fortunately for you, there are dozens, even hundreds of little wealth nuggets you can easily apply to your life to expand your portfolio and double, even triple your net worth.

Being smart with money and becoming wealthy is not rocket science, but for many it looks and feels like hard work. The funny thing is it, the fact of its very simplicity means that more and more people should know and be doing this. But they are not. This is because most people do not know how to make money work for them, not the other way around. This is also because making money involves patience and restraint. Everything about our culture advocates otherwise.

But do you want to end up broke by the time you retire? Do you constantly fend off phone calls from creditors? Do you sigh and shake your head at your bank balance? No one wants to spend their life waiting for payday and watching money flutter away the moment bills come in the mail.

Becoming wealthy is not just about falling into family money, inheriting a trust fund or even having a big income. In fact, many people with huge incomes rarely are truly wealthy. Huge incomes often equal huge expenses and struggling to keep your finances in the black every month does not equal financial freedom. Investing is different from spending. Someone who has a huge house or houses and a great car may look rich but may not be.

Are You Happy

Affluence and wealth can be hard to come by. If you are looking for secrets to getting millions or simply looking for a way to manage your money, this is it.

This book will teach you the secrets of the truly wealthy and is a step-by-step guide on how to get there. You will learn everything from gaining financial freedom to basic investing and secret tips from business giants all over the world.

True financial freedom is only a step away, if you know how. Are you ready to start becoming truly wealthy? These 77 gems and secrets are designed to help you turn your resources, whatever they may be, into true wealth.

Creating a Wealth Foundation: Earning Financial Freedom

The wealthy think differently. This is true and an inescapable fact. The otherthing is that there is a poor mindset and a wealthy one.

The rich have a different approach to life. They plan, risk and manage their money in a different manner. They also have a positive attitude towards life and opportunities. The first and most important step to true financial freedomis creating this mindset for yourself. This also involves a no-holds barred, honest look at your life and assets.

Creating a starting place is as important as moving forward, so it does not matter if you start with $1 or $1,000,000. It is all about the mindset and the willto move forward to creating your wealth.

1. Redefine what wealth means for you. Being "rich" simply is a term for many people. Technically, wealth or being wealthy is defined as having an abundance of resources or possessions. The high life does not equal wealth. Having a

gigantic mortgage for a beautiful home or a huge car payment does not equal wealth.

Are status symbols your end goal? Does wealth for you mean that ability not to worry about bills or how much is left in your checking account at the end of the month? Does it mean providing comfortably for your family or being free from financial worry? Does it mean the ability to afford luxury designer goods or getting a membership to the local country club? Being rich or being wealthy can also mean you enjoy a comfortable retirement.

Does wealth mean something totally different to you? Your definition of wealth goes a long way towards setting your goals.

2. Another important step when it comes to managing your wealth is to set goals. Start with an overall battle plan, such as "By the end of the year, I will have more at least $500,000 in savings." Why? You need to be a visionary to be wealthy. A common factor that sets the millionaire apart from the average Joe is this: they know they wanted to be wealthy and they were willing to take the steps to reach their goal.

To reach one goal, you have to make smaller goals and reach them. Every little step you take, every penny you save matters. Use smaller goals as stepping stones. For example, to save that $500,000, one needs to set aside $5000 every single month, invest or cut down expenses.

3. Manifest your financial destiny by setting your subconscious towards specific goals. Create dream charts by cutting out pictures of your dream status or words that empower to help fuel your subconscious and get you to wear you want to go. Never underestimate the power of your will and mind. Wealthy people never say they cannot do it, they think of ways so that they can.

Write it down. Seeing what you want, and getting what you want involve seeing it in black and white.

Are You Happy

4. Know how much you are worth. Take stock of all your assets and income and subtract your debt. Many people go through life financially blind, not knowing how much they are worth or how much they owe and often end up blindsided by money.

5. The test: Your age x (your average household income from all sources – inheritance) divided by 10 = your net worth. The rich have a net worth often double or triple the amount. The average American has less than half. The goal is to double your net worth.

6. The truly wealthy consider themselves as the foremost asset. Accordingly, they pay themselves first. They also tend to invest in themselves first, especially when it comes to education. Take classes and groom yourself to be the millionaire, entrepreneur and success you want to be.

7. Guard your ideas with the passion of the Secret Service. Commodities are now no longer limited to labor, but have expanded to include ideas, imagination and opportunities.

8. Keep in mind that the average millionaire is not who you think he is. The frugal rich stay richer—if you do not believe this, think of all those high flying celebrities who end up with their homes in foreclosure or selling their tell-alls on TV to pay for all that Cristal and all those houses.

The famous IKEA owner drives a Volvo. HSBC's chairperson famously goes around the main office turning off all the lights long after the employees have left. The stories go on and on. The rich do not live the lifestyle of the rich—they stay rich because they are frugal misers at heart.

9. Assess your income and what you can do with it. 80% of modern millionaires were able to get there on annual incomes of $55,000 or less. Even meager savings eventually add up to thousands or millions of dollars.

10. When you look at a job, always know how much the head honcho gets paid because this will later affect your income in terms of promotion, benefits and future potential earnings. If you are gunning for a six figure salary and the current CEO is getting by on $300,000 a year, then maybe the job is not for you.

11. Find alternative ways to generate income if you are unhappy about your current level of earnings or the amount of the salary you currently have. This can mean looking for other employment with better pay or benefits or finding ways to boost your income little by little. This can mean starting a cottage industry business, learning to invest, buying and selling online or any number of means to add to your nest egg.

12. Create forms of passive income, the type of income that you receive with little to no effort. Examples of this include: rent from property you own, licensing patents or dividends and returns from investments.

Passive income can come from many sources. Exploiting the business possibilities of the Internet through blogs or sales from eBay or Amazon is one way to add to your income with minimal effort. The truly wealthy prefer passive income anytime. It frees up time for you to do what you want, even while you earn.

13. Be diverse. Create streams of income, do not rely on one large river. A job that pays $3M is great, but an accident or sudden layoff can cut you off. Think outside your salary. A job paying you $1M a year, plus real estate profits that amount to $1M and another $1M from stock is a far easier and safer thing to manage.

14. Learn to hold off gratification. A wealthy person knows how to delay gratification and sacrifice the now for later. This often comes with a positive attitude towards work and wealth, such as: "If I invest now, I will make 10% more later."

The wealthy do not think of now, they think of the future. The present is merely an opportunity.

15. Change your mentality about spending. Do you really have to have that (place object here) now? The truly rich hold off gratification, knowing that what is trendy, popular or a must have today may not last until tomorrow.

16. Never be frightened of failure.

17. Be realistic. Growth and wealth do not appear overnight, unless you are lucky enough to win the lottery or find long lost treasure. Investments need time to mature and savings need time to accumulate. Patience will be well rewarded. The wealthy know that scrimping now will lead to better results in the future.

18. Create a sense of urgency in your life. Do not wait for things to happen to you. You may think that you are playing safe by waiting around or looking for the next big deal. This is the financial equivalent sitting around. Take risks, invest, start the business now. Seize opportunities the moment they happen. The first to get there often wins, leaving the losers in the dust.

Taking stock of what you have right now can have some advantageous surprises. For one, you may find out that you have more than you think. Second, it gives you a clear cut place to start and helps you find balance as well as set goals. After all, you cannot move forward without knowing where you come from.

Cutting Corners Where They Matter

When it comes to wealth generation, another important factor that is hard to follow is "living within your means." For many people, living in debt has become the norm. It is common for the average person to be buried in debt before they reach the age of 25. A consumer-driven economy based on floating credit also creates the impression that wealth means more products.

After taking a hard look at your assets and income, now you have to check your lifestyle and see where you can cut down on expenses.

19. Write down your expenses. Do not lie to yourself. There is nothing like seeing it in black and white (or red). Keep track of your expenses on a spreadsheet or if you prefer, in a notebook. It gives you a concrete idea of where you are spending too much and where you are spending too little.

If you are looking to save more, write down everything you buy and keep track of it. Do you really need to spend $5 a day on designer coffee? That amounts to $1800 dollars a year just on your morning cup of Joe. Is it paramount to have the latest car every single year when you are hip deep in auto loans?

20. Cut those credit cards. The average person owns at least seven cards. The average number you need to sustain a good to great credit score? The answer is one or two. One well-managed card does more for your credit score than the dozen overextended cards you have. If you can manage without one, why not cut them all? Your credit score is not just affected by cards, but by other loans you have in your name, like your mortgage or auto loan.

21. Ruthlessly cut out all the services you do not need and monitor those you do. One millionaire famously counted the sheets in toilet paper rolls because he thought suppliers were overcharging him. He was right.

22. Before you cut those cards however, understand the utilization ratio: the total credit used versus the total credit available to you. Many people keep multiple cards for fear that one or more lines will be cut, increasing the ratio over time. The goal is to have a very low ratio compared to debt, low balances and even lower interest.

23. Get a free copy of your credit report. Dispute any outdated items. Keep in mind that items should slide off, not

stay on. Focus on judgments, liens and any items that undermine your potential to lenders.

24. Understand how interest affects your debt. The wealthy understand how interest works for investments, for loans and how it compounds over time. Those who are not wealthy do not.

Compound interest is interest that is added to the principle at certain intervals on the debt. This means that the loan/balance of a certain loan gets higher over time and you end up paying more interest.

Compounding rates differ but can be legally done on a yearly, quarterly, yearly or even daily basis. A loan with a starting principal of $1000 charged with 20% interest per year turns into $1200 at the end of the first year and so on. In contrast, simple interest does not add to the principal of the loan, but is the amount charged for use of that money or loan.

25. PAY DEBT OFF ASAP. Pay more than the minimum on loans. Satisfy the interest and part of the principal—the debt amount will lessen over time and the bonus is you pay it off faster. The more you pay now, the less you pay later.

26. Keep records of any and all transactions over the Internet or phone, especially if you are fixing your finances.

    a. Print or save any changes to your account.
    b. When calling customer service, ask for the representative's employee number and record the time of the call in the event you need to follow up on a request.
    c. Keep exact files and amounts.
    d. Keep copies of everything.

27. Be hyper-vigilant when it comes to cards, loans or mortgages. Look for ways to lower interest, increase payments and keep an eye out for changes that could affect your loans.

28. Make a budget and stick to it. Think of it as a budge-it. Once you make it, you do not budge-it. Monthly and weekly budgets should be calculated to the penny.

29. The truly wealthy or those who want to be consider debt to be death to their portfolio. They only allow themselves to go into debt when they need it, and in that case they often refer to it as capital or even better, they often get it from someone else.

Keep the motto in mind when working with debt and get rid of it as soon as possible.

30. Separate your accounts to keep track of your money. Keep a savings account, an investment account and an earnings account.

31. Know the consequences of forbearing or deferring loans. The breathing room you get is often paid back threefold in capitalized interest or an increased loan principal.

32. Create an emergency fund or funds. These accounts should contain the equivalent of 3 to 6 months salary using low risk accounts (savings, certificates of deposits or insured money market accounts) as a safety net not just for your finances but for unexpected events in your life. This prevents you from dipping into your earnings or cashing in other income resources when unexpected and unwanted events happen, such as sudden illness.

33. Remember that you can grow rich now on money that you are throwing away. To be truly wealthy, you have to know that a simple dollar is an investment goldmine.

34. On average, millionaires spend more time selecting what to buy than buying the product itself. Why? Because they look for the best bargain before laying their money down—and ask for discounts before making a selection. Apply this principal to your life and watch your expenses go down.

Instead of selecting the first brand-name product you see, take the time to check what exactly you are getting. For example, many commercially branded cereal and grain products have exactly the same nutritional content as their generic cousins, at almost twice the price. Remember that you are paying more for the brand than you are for the product itself.

Millionaires and the wealthy also know the value of patience. Many stay in the first home they bought long after they can afford a more expensive one.

35. Never accept a deal at face value. Negotiate until you feel the terms are in your favor.

The most important thing you should know is that without financial freedom, you cannot be truly wealthy. The most important thing is to create a base: a lower debt to income ratio and leeway to save and put money aside for investing later on.

It also frees up your mind so you can implement the law of attraction. Implementing positive thinking in your life can draw in positive forces and create more and more goodwill and luck. It is hard to think positive when you are constantly worrying about bills or making payments. By thinking positive and creating more positivity in your life, you bring in not just monetary wealth but a wealth in your personal life as well.

Investing and Managing Your Wealth: Becoming Truly Wealthy

Once you have established a firm financial foundation or put aside a little money, it is time to learn to invest. Many first time investors fall into the trap of waiting, and waiting until they "have enough." The first thing you have to do is nix that notion, right now. You will find out by reading the tips that even measly amounts can add up to great amounts over time.

Others balk at investing because they think "I do not know enough to be a player." That is right. You do not. The truly wealthy understand how money works and never start sentences with the words "I do not know." If you do not understand investing and how it works, it is time to start to do the legwork.

Investing 101

The primary focus of investing is making your money work for you instead of working for your money. Many wealthy people have perfected the art of creating their wealth instead of giving a service. Building wealth also means creating wealth that is sustainable and continues to generate even in the event that you are unable to work.

36. Learn the difference between having a high income and being truly wealthy. High incomes do not necessarily mean that you are rich, especially if this income comes from only one source.

The myth persists that you can only be truly wealthy if you come into family money or are born into a home of silver spoons, silk sheets and antique furniture. Continue to believe in this myth, and you still have the mindset of the poor.

Many of the middle class believe that a high income job is the end all of their existence and work their butts off to get to a position that pays in five or six digits but end up baffled at how little they have by the time retirement rolls around.

For example, the average high level manager earns $200,000 a year, with benefits but stands to lose that income in the event of layoffs or illness. Although his income earning potential is high, it only comes from one source.

Contrast that with a middle level manager earning $50,000 a year. This middle manager, however, rents out properties in the city for another $500,000 and reaps dividends from stocks and bonds for another $100,000 a year. In the event of illness, death or mass layoffs, half of his earning potential is still secure.

The source of the latter's income is also easily passed on to future generations, securing wealth for the middle level manager's family.

37. Choose your investment goals as these will decide your allocation strategy later on. A broker or brokerage firm can help you decide on what your plans are, as well as help you begin investing.

38. Research the different types of investments as well as how risky they are. In general:

Stocks – you purchase partial ownership of a company and as part-owner, are entitled to annual profits. However, many people buy stock to sell when the price is high, not for dividends. The practice of buying low and selling high is relatively low risk but the potential for reward is governed by market and highly emotional changes. Yes, stock is considered an emotional asset.

Bonds – bonds are small loans to companies or governments that the investor pays for. They usually have fixed interest rates and are considered very safe and low risk investments. T-bills, municipal bonds and corporate bonds are some examples.

Mutual fund – this involves pooling money together with other like- minded investors to buy a full portfolio, usually run by firms or money managers. This type of investment is often the starting point for many first-time investors, simply because it provides a more diverse portfolio from the get-go.

REITS – these are companies that deal primarily with the ownership of real estate and manage a portfolio for you. They have the advantage of being diverse and easy to sell—as well as reduce the headache of managing your own property.

Other alternatives – Generally these are the high-risk and high reward securities where the payoff can be huge but the risk is high. Real estate, commodities, FOREX, options and futures fall under this category.

39. Create an allocation strategy for your savings or income to minimize risk and spread out your investments to guarantee several streams of income versus just one.

Learn about investing and accounting before you start spreading the money around. Consult with brokers or brokerage firm, especially if you have a lot to invest. Take night courses or read investment books to understand what you are getting into.

40. For example, you have $100,000 dollars to invest. 35% ($35,000) could go to property or real estate, another 30% for stocks, 10% for venture capital, etc. An allocation strategy helps you maximize your investments and also gives you the ability to indulge in some high-risk behavior, if you so wish, without losing all your capital. The financial equivalent of putting all your eggs in one basket, such as investing in all one type of equity, is portfolio suicide.

41. Support the traditional and explore the new. Opportunities grow with the growth of the Internet and the advent of technology. The Internet is not just a place to go to. The exponential growth of business and the changing face of technology creates more and more investment opportunities for the modern investor, as well as the modern entrepreneur.

42. Account for every cent, every nickel, every dime and quarter. The saying goes you never know the value of money until you have to dig around the couch cushions for it. The truly wealthy know that every penny can be put to good use. Money is stagnant only when you want it to be, or when it flies out of your hands.

43. Even small amounts matter. Many people say they will invest only when they have x amount, but even a small investment of $1000 can give you great returns in the future. By thinking of returns instead of instant cash or how much you have on hand, you create your wealth through possibilities.

Are You Happy

Saving 10,000 a year with a 10% rate of return and seeding that account with an additional 10,000 per year will yield $128,000+ after 10 years. If you start with $5,000, you end up with about $94,000 after said 10 years. That doesn't count the interest the account would generate for years after.

44. Invest your money as early as you can. The true friend of money is always time and the passage of it. The longer money sits and the more interest it collects, the higher the chances that you will reap thousands of dollars in returns.

A great example for this is the 401(k). Many Americans simply cannot wait until retirement and cash it in as soon as they can. But for what? A faster car, a bigger house or in some cases, that giant flat screen TV everyone else has.

Your 401(k) alone is a savings plan you must NEVER touch. Do the math. If you have an annual salary of $100,000 and contribute 10%, with a 50% employer match rate and no salary increases, you end up with $ 741,184.02 in 20 years.

Increase the contribution to 12%, with all other factors constant and the amount rises to $889,420.89. Increase the time frame to 30 years and you end up with $2 million.

45. Buy stock, not product. If you love the product, chances are others will to. So why waste time buying the product when you can make money off the stock. This creates a) passive income and b) a higher chance of return on investments.

Take Apple. Apple's stock has risen over 12 times in the past five years, quadrupling dividends for investors. How many iPhones or iPods have you bought over the past five years? How much money do you think an average shareholder has made from the products you have been buying? Even with the death of its founder, Steve Jobs, Apple's stock remained strong and rose.

Traditionally company stock falls with the death of visible CEOs or front men, but this was not true in this case.

One exception: keep in mind that sales do not make the stock. Activision is a company that markets and makes one of the biggest selling video games in the world, with sales totaling over 400,000 on the first day of the new installment release. However, their stock and shares have remained static for around 4 years.

46. Create assets that will make money for you with a minimum of effort. For example, investing in a restaurant does not require you to show up daily to manage the day-to-day running of the business, only to pay the management firm or keep the standard of a franchise.

47. Think long term. The truly wealthy do not count on single projects that net huge paychecks, but invest in opportunities that create returns and dividends that last for years. Long term also means the ability of securities to mature. Thinking long term means having the ability to see the future in a sense—and finding projects that affect and create these futures.

48. Do not wait for business opportunities, create them. Entrepreneurs look at an empty lot and see possibility and a method for them to get rich. Those with a poor mindset simply see an empty lot. The rich look at garbage and see a garbage hauling business, a rust-cleaning service, a recycling center. Those with a poor mindset see only the discarded tires, the dirt and the weeds.

49. Another great secret is to never care where you money comes from. Many people balk at investing in businesses that are not "sexy" perhaps because they do not want to tell people at parties that they got rich off sewage.

Truly wealthy people spread their money around and reap them in regardless if they were earned because of sewage or flowers. Who cares if it comes up in cocktail conversation?

50. Always think in terms of specific assets versus their overall value in the market. The truly wealthy do not rely on the ups and downs of the market, but the possible opportunities that stem from them.

For example, the real estate market may be down during the recession but right now savvy investors are buying up foreclosed property in great locations for half prices for later investment.

51. Know when to hold off, reassess and quit. Investors will say no. But not all of them will. Those with a poor mindset go to the bank for a loan, get rejected and never think about their idea or opportunity again. The wealthy mindset goes to the bank for a loan, gets rejected, redrafts the proposal and returns to get the approval.

The poor mindset goes into business not knowing the risks of the deal and is baffled when the fallout occurs. The wealthy mindset goes into a deal, knows the risk and gets out if things are going bad. Always follow your gut and do your research. Know when to back off from risky or unethical deals will not only take your money but have effects of your freedom.

52. Accept that there will be instances where you will experience some loss, such as when stock goes down or remains stagnant, therefore not providing you with the expected dividends. Accept that this will change as well.

53. Do not join the bandwagon: just because everyone is putting their money in it, does not mean you should. Get rich quick schemes are simply schemes.

54. Forget compartmentalizing your money. Every penny is important so do not think of it as a bonus or extra pay. The wealthy put every single cent to good use and are able to account for all of them.

The lesson here is to value every single dollar you earn. One millionaire started by investing $25, that is right, $25 in a mutual fund. He could not afford any more at the time, since he worked a menial job. As his pool grew, so did the amount of his investments. He is now worth multi-millions.

55. Learn about taxes and how to use them to your advantage, not the other way around.

56. The truly wealthy know how to make taxes work for them. Never be afraid to learn and ask. Instead of having someone do it for you, learn how to do it yourself.

57. Finally, never invest if you are not willing to wait. Otherwise, you are throwing your money away like a gambling addict at a poker table.

The truly wealth think of investing as a game that pays out and is a fun to play. Never for once think that they got there by simple luck. It takes a lot of research, studying and waiting to get there. The poor make excuses and say, they never have enough time between their jobs, their family and whatever other obligations they have.

The wealthy create the time to invest and invest in their time as well.

However, the main difference is this: they enjoy it. They enjoy the time they spend reading investment books. They enjoy reading the reports, watching the stock market and simply love the game of money. This is an attitude you need to become successful when you move to invest. This is the attitude that makes winners and makes the wealthy.

Making and Protecting Your Money

The average millionaire or comfortably wealthy person works for himself or owns a business. This is a law that is hard to follow. Most people think a business is a risky proposition simply because there are so many factors that affect the success of a business. A million things can go wrong, but a million things can also go right.

The wealth mindset is one that works for itself, cashing in on your own ideas and labor. The poor mindset works for others, laboring for a minimum cut of the profit.

The idea of working for yourself can be scary. Many first-time business owners fail because they sink everything they have into one venture and never recommit when the road to success gets rocky. The wealthy and the rich stick with their business plan and move forward regardless of the events, confident in their success.

    58.   Do something that you love, because you will never feel like it is work. The success stories of many entrepreneurs and millionaires always begin with this line "I love...[insert hobby, passion or interest here] so I…."

Money always follows passion and the upside is, you will never feel like you worked a day in your life. Ask yourself what you love to do, what you are good at and how important it is to you. Once you know what it is, you will know what venture to begin.

    59.   Alternatively, find a need for something you love and fill it. Filling a need or creating a need is an excellent starting point for a business. Curves Gym combined the owner's need for fitness and hatred of being ogled while at the gym.

She provided a women's only gym without mirrors, filling a need many women did not even know existed. Women lined up around the street to work out at this gym and it boasts hundreds of franchises around the US today.

    60.   Do not be afraid to do something humble—many a business has expanded from humble origins and cottage industries. No idea is too small, no business is "stupid".

61. Make sure your business fits your lifestyle. If you hate nightclubs, why start one? Why start a golfing business when you have never picked up a club in your life and have no interest in doing so?

62. Those who cannot run a business, invest in one. It takes the headache out of the management and gives you profit without the effort.

63. The wealthy know when to expand their business. Those who want to be truly rich run multiple businesses. Take Nigella Lawson, who started with a cooking show and now has a line of products and even utensils. One business, different umbrellas. Different umbrellas, one profit.

64. The business should never be static, but it should be familiar. Take a cue from top restaurants. They constantly change or update their menus but keep the customer favorites around.

65. Be the best. There are no exceptions to this rule. Provide the best service, the fastest delivery, the highest quality, the newest products. Follow these rules and the customers will come.

A sub rule to this secret is to always strive to continue to be the best. Once you have set a standard, customers and clients will expect you to maintain it. Many a business has experienced fallout after reaching heights due to declining service or worsening product. Take a cue from timeless products and services that continue to make money over the years. They never balk or shirk when it comes to quality. Even if it means making their customers pay a little extra.

66. Your business is defined by its employees— especially if you decide to go into any type of service industry. Hire for attitude, train for skill.

Never keep an employee who is not worth the salary you pay. Never tolerate stupidity, slowness or excuses. Instead, screen, evaluate and expect change. Millionaires never take slack from their employees. They never hesitate when the time comes to let one go.

67. Learn to recommit. Every business owner experiences fall out, bad sales or some sort of failure. There will always be a time when you fall into the red. It takes perseverance to go back into the black.

68. Economize where it counts. Find the best deals for raw product to maximize profit.

69. The truly wealthy know how to make profit with minimal expenditure. Reduce overhead, especially when it comes to trappings. A huge corner office with the antique desk and leather seats will not mean much when you are scrambling to pay the bills.

Protecting Your Money

Once you have money, you will take time to protect it by avoiding future catastrophes. Be cautious and always assume the worst. Do not go through life thinking that other people will not take advantage of you or that your money is not important to them. A careless mistake can cost you a fortune. A careless demeanor opens you up to attack. And you will never know where it is going to come from.

Now that you have the money, you have to take the steps to protect it from unscrupulous beings. Many a millionaire's downfall came from lawsuits from hungry money-grubbing relatives or the greed from immediate family. The media is packed with celebrity stories where the 'evil' spouse gets millions in the divorce, millions they never earned simply because the high earner took no precautions.

In the case of lawsuits, anything personal amounts to what you or your companies are worth. Lawyers love public information and can easily figure out what you are worth by accessing public records. Transferring the bulk of your wealth to foundations, trusts or corporations ensures that these stay well out of the public's eye or are untouchable in the event you are attacked.

Protecting your money now ensures that it will continue to benefit you and your family for years and decades to come.

70. Millionaires and the truly wealthy never put assets in their name and guard their personal assets zealously. They use corporations and protect themselves with liability insurance. Corporate entities are used to operate businesses, partnerships are made with the idea that if all goes to hell, it is time to get out Use trusts, family partnerships and protect your personal assets and wealth.

71. Turn yourself into a stealthy, moving target. Never be conspicuous about your wealth and forego the trappings of it. Remember: the bigger, flashier bird is always easier to bring down. The birds that fly low, fly below the radar and detection.

72. Begin asset protection early to prevent any mishaps. Never let yourself get caught in the trap of beginning asset protection when you are already in heaps of trouble!

There is nothing like being prepared. Besides, transferring assets when you are being sued is illegal and can land you in jail (plus you lose everything). Protect your personal assets from claims and unscrupulous parties!

73. Create a clear-cut and legal will, even if you are only 32 years old. Make sure you know where your money is going. Many people put off the idea of the will simply because it makes them face their own mortality which is always wrong.

Update and notarize yearly, or anytime you like. A will prevents many a family feud, protects your interests long after you are gone and ensures that money that you share keeps going where you want it go. Without a will, chaos will ensue, especially if your personal fortune and business assets are worth six digits or more.

For businesses, the equivalent of a will is known as succession planning. Many successful business have failed because an epic predecessor was not able to carefully plan who would succeed him in the event of his death.

Follow the example of Steve Jobs and create a succession plan for your business before you even get sick or retire. Many family corporations create a version of this by grooming successors from within the family and stipulating conditions to be met in order to inherit or run the business.

74. Never enter any partnership, including conjugal ones, without a back-up plan or a clear way out. That is what prenuptial agreements are for. Do not let a future ex-spouse pull a Paul McCartney on you.

75. Never put all your money into one humungous deal. Diversity is the key to true wealth. Keep in mind that those eggs in one basket are more liable to break if the basket is too heavy.

76. Once you become wealthy, do not forget the rules and secrets that got you there. First time millionaires and lotto winners often blow through their millions by acquiring status symbols like mad and often end up with nothing. Continue to extol the virtues that got you to where you are now. Live simply and below your means, even if you are worth enough to make it to the Forbes 500 list.

77. The final timeless wealth secret. Money is meant to shared, not hoarded. Follow the Rockefeller rule: 10% of your worth is meant to shared. This creates more for you.

Conclusion

There is no shortcut to instant wealth. Being rich means playing a game that lasts for years. The truly wealthy not only look forward to this game, but also look forward to playing it. By following these timeless secrets, you learn the value of hard work, patience and reap the rewards for years to come.

Never be complacent and put off your wealth creation for tomorrow. True wealth and real wealth starts by making these changes today. Break that piggy bank and start investing now.

Wealth creation is both a complex strategy and a waiting game but by following these 77 tips, you can be on your way to true wealth, a comfortable lifestyle and living your life financially free.

Are You Happy

You can find All of the answers to the fun Word searches, Word Scrambles and Matching pages at

www.MLRuscsak.com

About the Author

Finding the CEO in You

Melisa is all about authenticity, as anyone who's met her can attest. Whether you've seen her speak or talked with her at an event, or had a conversation with Melisa she is relaxed and candid. In the same way, her speaker bio doesn't just share the standard info about her credentials and speaking skills

"Motivational Keynote Speaker, Melisa Ruscsak works with individuals and organizations to amplify their communication, connection, and confidence so they can make an influential impact on the world. She mentors with passion, guiding her clients to effectively strengthen and elevate their leadership vision to new heights.

With over five years of corporate training experience, a knack for making meaningful connections with audiences, and an insatiable appetite for helping others maximize their potential, Melisa knows how to rock a platform, connect with a crowd and provide training so that others can effectively do the same.

Melisa's down-to-earth humor compels audiences to laugh while they learn. She engages groups from the moment she steps in front of them and leaves them with empowering tools and focused mindsets that they will use long after the lights have gone out on the event. Melisa is passionate about people, leadership, and successful businesses. She is especially inspired to help people take their careers - and themselves - to unprecedented levels.

When not speaking or training, Melisa can be found creating new worlds and stories within her literary world. Those works can either be found in stories for young adults or housed within screenplays.
- Mini Biography By: RC Management and Publishing Services

Connect with Melisa at

[M. L. Ruscsak (facebook.com)](#)

[Melisa Ruscsak (@mlruscsak) • Instagram photos and videos](#)

[Melisa Ruscsak (@RuscsakMelisa) / Twitter](#)

[M. L. Ruscsak - YouTube](#)

[M. L. Ruscsak | Trient Press](#)

[Home | Dove & Dragon Radio (doveanddragonradio.com)](#)

[Melisa Ruscsak - IMDb](#)